Table of Contents

Dark Manipulation Emotional Control

Introduction

Chapter 1: Mastering your emotions

Chapter 2: Emotional Intelligence

Chapter 3: Boosting Emotional Intelligence

Chapter 4: Self-Confidence

Chapter 5: The Power of Neurolinguistics Program

Chapter 6: Mind Manipulation-Persuasion

Chapter 7: Hypnosis techniques

Conclusion

Description

Introduction

Emotions are an important part of human existence. If you didn't know, the general look of things is a result of human emotions just like it is of human intellect. Emotions can reveal feelings to the mind and define a want, or a need, and the mind processes the need and causes the person to respond to the emotion.

The method of influencing people through emotional confusion is the most popular one and is pretty easy to do. It basically plays a role in eliminating logic from the conversation. Logic makes the person think and the last thing you would want your target to do is to think because it can interfere with manipulation. What you want is to steer the conversation to a place where he or she is an emotional state so their ability to think rationally is destroyed.

Most people consider emotional manipulation as regularly invoking strong emotional states to eliminate the logic from the situation. However, that is not always the case, you need to choose the right time to invoke that strong emotional desire. If you keep on switching between strong emotional states, it will only confuse your target and prevent you from achieving your ideas. That said, let us dive in and explore more on emotional manipulation.

Chapter 1: Mastering your emotions

Emotions can be compared to waves, you cannot stop them from coming, but we can decide which one to surf.

So, do you have what it takes to take charge of your emotions?

Are you aware that your daily emotional experience determines the decisions you make and the actions you take?

It is said that it is not what happens to us, but how we react to what happens, that defines the outcomes you will get in your life. And the way you respond is directly determined by how you decide to interpret the events and situations of your life. This similarity starts from your potential to properly control your emotions in ways that will allow them to serve and help you attain your desired results.

Each of the negative emotions that we experience daily can help us and provide us with the necessary guidance we deserve to make effective decisions throughout the day. For this reason, it is paramount that we spend the time to learn how to interpret our emotions in ways that will assist us in finding solutions, not challenges.

This chapter will present you with the necessary knowledge you need to control and interpret your emotions far more effectively throughout the day. First, let us take a look at the limiting emotions that we experience every day.

Unmasking emotional types

In this section, we shall look at ten universal emotions that most of us tend to experience throughout our lives.

It is essential to understand that these emotional responses trigger your conscious brain that something isn't working and thus, something needs to change. In other words, they are a call to action, guiding you to do something specific to eliminate your pain.

Lastly, all the emotions discussed here are a result of stuck-states that happen to us throughout the day. These stuck-states are patterned responses to people, events, and circumstances that have their physiological phrases, and words. They are comfort-seeking methods that we apply when thing don't go as planned or the way we expected.

Here is a breakdown of the ten emotional states.

Discomfort

This is an uncomfortable emotion that triggers boredom, impatience, and distress.

You could be experiencing discomfort because you are interpreting a situation or a set of events in a certain wat that naturally results in you feeling pain. It is within this interpretation that discomfort happens. This, then, means that once you change your description of the event, you gain control over your emotional experience.

If you ever experience this emotion, it is crucial first to identify what is it that you are doing, and secondly how exactly you are interpreting your experience or reality. If what you are doing is not generating the results that you expect, then try taking a new approach. However, if you aren't able to handle the situation from a different perspective, then to change your perspective on the job. Either way, you need to find a response that will assist you to pull yourself out of this uncomfortable emotional state.

Take, for example; you experience boredom, then try something new. Or you can try and interpret your experience in a unique way by changing things into a game. Either strategy will work well as long as you are ready to be flexible in your technique.

Hurt

The emotion of pain always makes us feel powerless and leads to a sense of jealousy and loss. You might be experiencing hurt because you interpret a turn of events in a certain way that makes you feel hurt. Similarly, feeling hurt could be a result of not communicating your needs properly to others. Therefore, you need to start today to express what you need from your relationships in an open and non-threatening way.

If telling others your needs doesn't work, then consider your expectations. Probably your expectations aren't reasonable, it could be that they have changed over time, or they no longer apply to your present relationship and thus may have to be reevaluated.

Lastly, feelings of hurt may happen from a lack of understanding of our relationships. In this case, it helps if you replace your pain with curiosity and fascination. By getting curious, you instantly start to ask better questions, which widens the way you think and leads to responses and possibilities that you might not have factored before.

Guilt

Guilty may leave you feeling deflated and typically results in the emotion of regret.

You feel guilty because you interpret a situation in a different wat that stimulates the feeling of guilt. And the longer you hold onto that guilt, the worse it becomes as it continues to grow inside your head.

When you experience guilt, it is important to understand that experience of sin is as a result of our interpretation of what we did or failed to do and the effect this has had on others. Once you decide to interpret the events and situations of your life uniquely, you will realize that guilt immediately vanishes and becomes something that can motivate and inspire you to take positive action.

Fear

Fear is a debilitating emotion that results in anxiety, indecision, and worry.

You could be experiencing fear because you interpret a situation in a way that makes you feel fearful. This feeling of alarm arises from an emotional response to what may happen in the future if you take a specific action. This is all well-and-good if it is something that is meant to protect you from any harm. But in many cases, our fears are grappled with inaccuracies that mislead us. As such, the first thing you must always do to eliminate anxiety from your life is to separate the "real" from the "imagined."

Fear, is, of course, a critical emotion because it protects us from danger. However, in this modern day-and-age, it always harms us because it prevents us from accomplishing our goals and objectives.

Anger

Anger tends to get out of control and can always lead to resentfulness.

Anger can also serve us if we can understand its underlying meaning.

Before you quickly embrace the emotion of anger, it is important to note that anger always arises because one or more of our rules has been broken by others. Thus, we get angry because we no longer feel in control of the situation or circumstances. In this case, we can always let go off anger quickly by taking the time to examine our rules. Maybe they are not realistic, or they are out-of-date, or they don't need to be applied in these situations.

Similarly, anger can arise because of wrong interpretation of situations, or people's intentions. In this case, you must ask whether or not you have misinterpreted the job or misinterpreted people's intentions. Be open and passionately look for alternative meanings. It is only a flexible and open approach that will generate the answers you want.

Frustration

Frustration is one of those emotions that we love to hate because it causes us to feel like we are so close, yet so far away from the result we want.

You are getting frustrated because you are interpreting a situation in a way that naturally causes you to feel frustrated. It is within this feeling that your responses lie.

You can be frustrated because you are trying hard to do something, but you don't get the results you expect. It is like someone is holding you back from your goal by some external force that you cannot control.

Rather than attempt to control the situation, the secret is to start thinking outside the box, to begin considering new possibilities, solutions, and ideas that might very well assist you in solving the problem you are dealing with. Sometimes, all it takes is for you to review new information that will generate the insight you need to see the situations from a different perspective.

Lastly, frustration happens from not achieving the results you are after. In this case, all it takes to resolve your failures is to change your approach. Try something new and different that you had not considered before. Curiosity, flexibility, and determination approach are the secrets you should be looking for.

Disappointment

This is the feeling of not getting what you want and always arises from a sense-of-defeat.

When you feel disappointed, you always wish that things could have been different. But, we cannot change the past while we can modify our past experiences in a positive way.

Rather than swimming in disappointment, decide instead to learn from your experiences so that you can improve yourself in the future. Other times, it is even essential to look for opportunities that may be available because of the disappointment that you have just experienced.

Disappointment can always be as a result of having unrealistic expectations that can rarely be accomplished. In that case, change your expectations by limiting them to a level that can be realistically achieved. This could probably remove you from the pit of disappointment.

Inadequacy

Inadequacy can make you feel unworthy and incompetent. It is an emotion that leaves you feeling like you are at the bottom of the heap with no means out.

You are experiencing inadequacy because you don't have the experience, knowledge, or skills to live up to your high expectations. So you can either renew your expectations about yourself and your ability, or you can step out there and acquire the required knowledge, skills, and experience to attain the outcomes you want to have in your life.

You could also experience inadequacy because you undermine your strength and abilities. In such situations, it is vital to get a second opinion. Thus, step out there and ask someone for feedback. Ask them to give honest observations. Maybe they will deliver surprising insights and perspectives.

Finally, inadequacy can always arise from a lack of confidence. If you have low self-esteem, then it is entirely right to feel inadequate. But if you take the time to build your confidence, then you will enhance your self-belief and start to feel better about yourself and your prospects.

Overwhelm

Virtually, everyone at one point in life experience overwhelms, and before they realize it, it takes over their lives and sometimes can lead to debilitating emotions of depression and grief.

You can experience overwhelm because you have a lot on your plate or you are unable to control certain aspects of your life. In this case, you feel out of control and unable to react accordingly.

The answer to overwhelm lies controlling small chunks of your life, one part at a time. It means taking a fraction of your life and dividing it up into smaller manageable sections that you can successfully work with. It also means letting go of any unnecessary commitments that are pulling you behind, or rescheduling them in a way that will free up your time and while giving you more space to do what is most important.

Managing to overwhelm is quite simple if you know what to do and are committed to taking the actions required to reschedule your life accordingly. Sometimes, all it takes is a small lesson in productivity.

Loneliness

Loneliness is a dangerous emotion that can lead to sadness.

You could be experiencing loneliness because you are looking at life in a way that is different from what lies outside of you.

So the way to conquer loneliness is to network with your friends, reconnect lost friendship and reconnect with everything in your surroundings.

Lastly, don't forget the things that you are grateful for, always look back and appreciate those things whoever small they may be. By doing this way, you will recover the balance you have been missing in life. And this gratitude will motivate you to share your secrets with others.

Chapter 2: Emotional Intelligence

Do you want to learn how to manage your emotions and remain calm even in stressful conditions? Are you interested to learn how to control your feelings of anger and frustration, so you don't snap at friends and colleagues when things don't go your way?

The ability to learn and control your emotions is known as emotional intelligence. And the higher your emotional intelligence is, the more likely you are to succeed in your career, communicate effectively at work, and have a better relationship.

What is Emotional intelligence

Emotional intelligence, also known as your ability to track and manage your emotions, and appreciate and impact the feelings of others.

People with advanced emotional intelligence don't allow their emotions to move their actions. They know when their emotions are about to move to the deep end, and, most importantly, they know to use those emotions, so they don't negatively affect anyone else.

Emotional intelligence is a mix of personality traits. The psychologist who invented the field of emotional intelligence highlighted five main aspects that define emotional intelligence.

That includes:

1. Self-awareness
2. Empathy
3. Self-regulation
4. Social skills
5. Motivation

Emotional intelligence is something that occurs with being human, at least to some degree. Some people are born with a higher level of emotional intelligence, while others try hard to understand why they feel the way they do, and can't seem to understand when another person is having a bad day.

The great thing is that while emotional intelligence is a combination of personality of traits, they are all characteristics that can be improved with practice and discipline. This implies that all of us can work to enhance EQ.

Benefits of emotional intelligence

It is believed that emotional intelligence is more important than IQ. The reason is that in most cases, intelligence alone can only get an individual far.

A high IQ will not help you attain your goals, work successfully with a team, have a better relationship, or even work well in stressful situations.

On the other hand, emotional intelligence can help you succeed in all spheres of your life.

1. Greater job satisfaction and performance

A study released in the Leadership Quarterly discovered that professionals with a higher EQ experienced more job satisfaction and had a higher performance level than those with a lower EQ score. In a separate study released in the Journal of Organizational Behavior, it also concluded that the higher your EQ, the better your job performance becomes.

Higher satisfaction in the job positively improves your general happiness, especially when you spend most of the waking time at work. Additionally, better work performance can result in more promotions and raises in the whole career.

Talent Smart measured emotional intelligence besides 33 other workplace skills and discovered that emotional intelligence was the best predictor of performance, representing 58% of success in job types. Also, they say that 90% of all high performers have strong emotional intelligence.

2. Improved relationships

Emotional intelligence can result in a better relationship with your spouses, partners, friends, and children. It can still help you to create better business relationships with your colleagues, boss, and clients.

A study released in the Journal of Personality and Individual Differences discovered that those with a higher EQ revealed more satisfaction in their relationships, and lower negative associations with close friends.

Emotional intelligence provides one with the ability to link deeply with others through active listening, compassion, and empathy.

3. Less workplace stress

A study released in The International Journal of Organizational Analysis discovered that people with higher emotional intelligence experience low workplace stress compared to those with lower EQ scores. People with higher

EQ scores strongly committed to their organization.

Why? It could be a mix of several factors. In general, those with a higher EQ score revealed a deeper relationship with colleagues. They also don't allow toxic coworkers to impact their happiness and productivity. These two elements can highly limit work stress.

4. Better self-control

Anyone can get angry-that is pretty easy. However, to get angry with the right individual, to the right level, at the right time, for the correct purpose, and in the right way, is not that easy.

If you get angry quickly at the smallest things or snap at your children when things fail to go your way or find yourself annoyed as you wait for the traffic to end, you aren't alone. Everyone experiences a problem controlling their emotions and keeping fresh in difficult situations.

The challenge is that anger can make you commit a big mistake, both to you and to others, especially when it is uncontrolled. However, it doesn't have to go this way. Just like Aristotle once said, self-control and understanding are important to controlling anger and channeling it where it can do the best.

Enhancing your emotional intelligence will boost your self-control, and allow you to understand strong emotions better so you can control it appropriately.

5. More happiness

No one can make you feel small without your permission.

People with a higher level of emotional intelligence understand what makes them happy, and, most importantly, they don't allow others to prevent their happiness. They know that they, and they alone, can manage their emotions.

This strong realization not only results in greater inner strength, but it can also still lead to greater happiness and feelings of general well-being-and research supports this up. A study released in the journal Personality and Individual Differences defines that emotional intelligence is related to positive life results and greater well-being.

The 5 Important Components of Emotional Intelligence that will assist you achieve

Emotional Intelligence refers to how an individual controls their personality to be personally and interpersonally effective. It is their potential to examine, assess, and control one's emotions, the emotion of others, and that of groups.

It is the difference between a manager or a leader or a task-driven person. Experience reveals that when you lack this important skill, you can demotivate and become less effective at what you do.

Persons with a higher level of emotional intelligence understand what they are feeling, what their emotions mean, and how these emotions can impact others.

Daniel Goleman-an, an American psychologist who helped promote emotional intelligence, defines five important aspects of emotional intelligence:

Higher emotional intelligence boosts relationships lead to the development of problem-solving skills and enhance the rise of new strategies.

Goleman breaks it down as the potential to assess, examine, and control one's own emotions, the emotions of others and that of groups.

Facts based on emotional intelligence

Neurological evidence reveals that feelings and thoughts do not happen randomly. They are responses to a stimulus which has been interpreted, perceived and filtered via a person's underlying attitudes. It is an individual's attitude that highly affects their thoughts, feelings, and behaviors. Consequently, Emotional Intelligence is mainly affected by attitudes.

1. Self-Awareness

Practically this means understanding that you are the changes of emotional state. For instance, when a single mention something to you that angers you. Emotional intelligence people will be aware that for instance, their heart is pumping faster. That feeling in the pit of their stomach exists and finally that they now choose to respond to the situation. In particular, those rich in Emotional Intelligence decide how they respond; they are under massive control.

Self-awareness has a lot of benefits, including the ability to discover problems that emerge so that you can deal with them swiftly-before they grow bigger. Also, it provides one with the potential to see things from a more explicit angle, ensuring that your response to emotions is better.

Individuals with an advanced level of emotional intelligence are comfortable with their own emotions and thoughts and know-how they affect others. Understanding and accepting how you feel is always the first step to overcoming.

People with greater self-awareness are confident in themselves, and their abilities and know-how others perceive them.

Self-awareness in emotional intelligence

- Accurate self-assessment: Recognizing the strength and limits of an individual.

- Emotional awareness: Understanding one's emotions and their effects.

- Self-confidence: sureness concerning one's self-worth and potential.

Self-regulation

Self-regulation involves showing your emotions correctly. It is also important to control and manage your emotions. A strong self-regulation skill means that you are concerned about how you affect others and take charge of your actions.

Slamming the phone down in front of your team demonstrates a lack of self-regulation and that you have failed to identify the effect of your behavior on your team.

Behaving in a way that you aren't careful can result in mistakes being made and can destroy relationships with colleagues.

It is important to realize that controlling your emotions does not mean you destroy things. This will only create additional stress — self-regulation demands that you wait for the correct time, and place to show your emotions.

Experts in self-regulation are flexible and adaptable to change. They are also experienced in handling conflict and finding solutions for complex situations.

Self-Motivation

We all respond well to positive people with a passion, and there is no difference when it comes to leadership. Being motivated as a leader means that you respond to a vision. Emotional intelligent individuals are passionate about work and will extend past money. In their hearts, they may want to build a better world so that they improve themselves.

Persons with these motivational skills can conquer failure and look for ways to move forward. People with this type of mental ability tend to make great leaders.

A passion for you what you do is important for your emotional intelligence. This results in better decision making and a better understanding of the plans of the organizations.

Empathy

Empathy refers to how you associate with others and know-how they may feel. Those two things are important traits which will not only make a person happier and successful but also those around you.

Responding to others, emotions are vital. Detecting a specific mood or emotion from a client and reacting to it can go a long way in enhancing your relationship.

Great skills in empathy can assist you in organizing a conversation and a presentation. You should apply empathy in business and sales. Learning the emotions of an individual that are required is important in responding to the needs and selling whatever you want.

If you are a leader, empathy can assist you in living with compassion and considering how others feel.

There are three types of empathy

1. Cognitive empathy

This refers to awareness or understanding someone else's point of view. It is a critical aspect of ensuring better communication and connection.

2. Social empathy

Here, you assume yourself what the other person is feeling. To build rapport, pay total attention to the other individual.

3. Empathic concern

Empathy in emotional intelligence

- Empathy: Consider others' feelings and point of view, and take an active interest in their needs.
- Service orientation: Recognize, anticipate, and fulfill customers' needs.
- Leveraging diversity: Create opportunities through diverse people.
- Political awareness: Understanding a group's power relationships and emotional currents.

Social skills

Building rapport, getting well with people is important in leadership and makes life full in private lives. Great social skill is an advantage besides the four emotional intelligence traits.

In the work environment, social skills enhance communication. It benefits those working by building connections and relationships. Some critical social skills involve verbal communication skills, active listening, persuasiveness, and leadership.

Applying social skills to win new business is part of enhancing rapport and improving communication between client and organization.

"friendliness with a purpose," involves treating every individual with respect and politely.

Social skills in emotional intelligence

Team capabilities: Building energy in seeking collective goals.

Leadership: guiding and inspiring people and groups.

Conflict management: resolving agreements

Influence: developing effective strategies for persuasion.

Change catalyst: Managing change

Collaboration and cooperation: working with others toward a common goal

4. Social awareness

Being socially aware refers to the way you respond to various social situations and properly change your interactions with other people so that you can attain the best results.

It also involves knowing the world around you and how different environmental impact people. Increasing social awareness implies enhancing your skills to link with others nonverbally, verbally, and in the community.

Social skills you weren't taught in school

Self-awareness

Before you can do anything, you need to know what your emotions are. Enhancing your self-awareness is the first step to highlighting any problem area you are encountering. Below are some tips for using to enhance self-awareness:

Set up a journal: Have a journal to help you monitor your emotions. Note down what happened to you, how you felt, and how you handled it. Regularly, check your diary and highlight any trends, or any time you reacted badly to something.

Request input from others: When addressing self-perception, suggestions from other people can be critical. Try to find out from people who know you well about your strengths and weaknesses. Note down what they say, now compare what they say, and identify for some patterns. But ensure that you don't argue with them. It is not a must for them to be correct. You are merely attempting to measure your perception from a different perspective.

Meditate: Emotions are likely to get out of control when you don't have time to process them. The next time you emotionally react to something, try to pause before you respond. You can also attempt to meditate to slow your brain down and provide your emotional state space to breathe.

If you have never taken time to practice intentional self-awareness, these tips should provide you with a great head start. One approach that many people like to use is to go on long walks or talk to yourself. Typically, you will realize that the things you say to your imaginary another end of the conversation can provide you with insight into what is disturbing you. The most important element is gaze inwards instead of only external elements.

Self-management

Once you understand the way your emotions operate, you can begin to figure out how to deal with them. The correct self-management implies managing your outbursts, differentiating your external triggers and internal over-reactions, and doing what is right for your needs.

One critical method to control your emotions is to divert your sensory input. You have perhaps heard of the old advice where you are required to count to ten and breathe when you are feeling angry. Speaking like an individual who has had a lot of troubling problems with depression and anger, this advice is crap. Despite that, providing your physical body with a jolt can end the cycle. If you are feeling lethargic, you need to perform some exercise. In case you are stuck in an emotional loop, then you need to give yourself a break. Anything that will provide a small shock to your system can help.

You should also try to funnel emotional energy into something productive. It is okay to allow overwhelming emotions to brew inside you for a moment if it is not the correct time to let them out. But when you do, rather than complain, convert it into motivation.

It is hard to control what makes you feel a certain way, but you can always regulate how you respond. If you experience an impulse control problem, look for methods to find help when you are feeling calm. Not all emotions can be eliminated. Some emotions persist long after the overflow. But there is a time when those feelings appear a bit intense. So you need to use that time to seek help.

Motivation

Motivation is a topic that is discussed a lot. When talking about motivation about emotional intelligence, we don't just simply get the energy to rash to work. It is an inner drive to achieve something. That drive isn't just feel-goody nonsense, either. There is a part of your prefrontal cortex that ignites the thought of realizing a critical goal.

Whether you aim to build a career, raise a family, or build a kind of art, everyone needs something they want to achieve with their life. When your motivation is working for you, it relates to reality in many ways. If you're going to have a family, then you need to start dating, that is what motivated people always do. Do you want to improve your career? Motivated people teach themselves, search for new jobs, or look for a promotion.

Before you can begin to use motivation, you need to look for your values. Many people are so busy that we have no time to look for our values. Or even worse, we can do what directly opposes what we value most that we end up losing the motivation completely.

Empathy

Your emotions are just half of all your relationships. It is the half you concentrate on the most, but that is because you spend most of your time with yourself daily. All other people that are important to you have their desires, feelings, and fears. Empathy is your most critical skill for overcoming your relationships. Understanding is a permanent skill, but there are a few tips you can apply to practice empathy.

- **Take a different position to your own:** This is the quickest approach to enforce an opinion in your mind. To argue against it, take a separate stand. If you believe your boss is unreasonable, try to defend their actions. Do you find their choices absurd when you are in their shoes? Even asking the questions yourself can allow you to emphasize with another perspective.

- **Keep quiet and listen:** It is hard to experience everyone else's lives to understand them completely, but still you have a chance to attend. Listening demands that you allow the other person to talk and then not opposing what they say. This means you set aside your opinions, or preconceptions for some time and give the other person you are talking to an opportunity to say how they are feeling. While it is challenging to practice empathy, every relationship you experience can at least be enhanced by waiting for some seconds before retaking the conversation.

- **Don't just be aware, attempt to understand:** Understanding is the primary goal of empathy. Understanding is the distinction between knowing something and empathizing with it. When a person tries to narrate about an experience that is not your own, spend time to think about how your life may be different if you experienced that daily. It is okay if you don't spend all your time focusing on someone else's life, but dedicating some little time while you work can be important.

Social skills

Social skills take many different forms-it is more than just being able to chat. These abilities extend from being able to assume how another person is feeling of becoming a great team player. All the skills you need to become socially competent are acquired in life. We can improve on any of them we are concerned about, but it requires time, effort, and perseverance. It okay to have a model, someone who exemplifies the skill we want to enhance. But we also need to practice anytime a naturally occurring chance arises.

You can begin with the most common social problem: resolving a disagreement. This is the point where you get the chance to test all your skills in a real-world scenario. Here is a basic summary of this topic:

- Determine the emotions and deal with them: Anytime you get into an argument, things can always get heated. If a person involved is emotionally worked up, then you need to address that issue first. Spent some time to vent before you can return to the problem. In a work setting, this could imply complaining to a friend before email your boss back. In a romantic relationship, this could mean letting your partner that you care about them before you point a finger. Additionally, never tell someone to "stay calm." This can worsen things.

- **Address important issues once you remain calm.** Once you are in your correct headspace, find out what the conflict is. Before you get to solutions, ensure that you and the other person agree on what the issues are. Develop solutions that are beneficial and sympathetic to any concessions the other individual may not be ready to make.

- **Finish on a cooperative style:** In business and any other setting, relationships work well when every member knows that they are on the same page. Even when you cannot finish on a definite style, ensure that the last intention you channel is a cooperative one. Allow your significant other to understand that you are striving towards the same goal, even if you have different opinions.

Not every interaction with someone else will end in conflict. Some social skills demand that you encounter new people every day, interacting with persons of different ideologies, or even playing games. But resolving conflict can be one of the best approaches to learn how to use your emotional skills. Conflicts are best corrected when you understand what you want and can communicate it clearly, know what another person wants, and come to favorable terms for everyone. If you are keen, you will realize that this involves every sphere of emotional intelligence model.

12 ways of improving customer service

1. Use positive motivation habits

Everyone has that inner critic that will want to prevent you from doing something, to make this critic less powerful and at the same time, inspire yourself to take action and increase your self-esteem. It is important to apply positive motivation habits.

Some that you can use to replace the inner critic include:

- Remind yourself of the gains. A simple but excellent method to inspire yourself and ensure that motivation continues is to write down the deeply felt benefits you will attain from this new path.

For instance, getting into the right shape and having sufficient energy for your kids and the people around you and or making enough money to travel with loved ones and experience beautiful things together.

Once you have compiled your list, save it and put it somewhere where you will see it daily. This can be in your workplace or your fridge.

- Concentrate on doing what you love to do. When you like to do something, enjoy doing something, then the desire to do that thing tends to come naturally. When you want something in life, then it also becomes easier to push through any inner resistance you may feel. Thus, if you lose your desire, ask yourself: Am I doing what I want to do? If not and if possible, try to concentrate and work on that very important thing.

Once you have applied your stop word, concentrate on one of these strategies. With time, it will become a habit, and your inner critic will pop up more often.

2. Learn new things

When you have enough knowledge about things, and you learn, you increase the information base that provides you with confidence. We could be tempted to outsource our learning to technology, relying on smartphones for all our information, and, indeed, we can never know everything, but learning new things raises our confidence. Not just that you know something, but you have done something significant that you can measure and recognize.

3. Master something

When you get well and proficient at something, it improves your self-confidence because you have the skills. The point is, we can all get well at whatever we want and many of us if we want to dedicate the effort to become experts. Expertise is a field that allows us to overcome imposter syndrome and results in higher self-confidence.

4. Get a few wins

When we attain small successes, it builds a positive narrative in our lives that can improve us and even result in greater challenges. When we win, we begin to believe that we can win, and this belief lies in our ability to succeed- it breeds higher confidence. So you should look for some small things you know you can succeed at and do them to increase your self-confidence.

5. Use positive language

The way we speak to ourselves is important because it is part of our belief narrative. When we speak negatively, it sets a negative perception, and probably works against our confidence. When we speak positively, it creates a belief narrative that works with confidence instead of against it.

Find and note down positive statements that you can speak to yourself to build that positive and confident persona.

6. Question you're critical thoughts

We all have critical thoughts that speak to us. These are times when we negatively perceive ourselves. But a lot of times, those critical thoughts don't depend on reality. It is critical to analyze these thoughts to learn when they don't have a basis in reality. If you critically analyze your negative perceptions and then take a sensible view of them, you will realize that many of them are false. When you recognize that these thoughts aren't true, it is a huge step to attaining greater confidence.

Understand that most negative thoughts occur on autopilot, and don't reflect the reality but occur because of past conditioning. Your lack of self-confidence may be because of negative thinking that has no basis in fact. To evaluate those thoughts to learn what is real and what's not.

7. Enhance your appearance

Our self-presentation is a way of nonverbal communication, not only with others but with ourselves. What we put on, our level of fitness and our grooming shows the extent of our inner attitudes and perceptions about ourselves. Thus, changing your appearance in a reverse manner can also divert your thoughts and perceptions. The feelings, as it is, come after the actions.

So, you should work out, dress well, eat healthily, groom yourself, etc. All these things send a message to your inner self and assist in changing that thinking into a positive and confident self-concept. Your outward appearance is a non-verbal message to yourself.

8. Pay attention to your posture and gestures

In the same way, the way you conduct yourself and how you change your body is a means of nonverbal communication. How you stand, what you do with your hands, how you sit, and how you speak are all forms of nonverbal communication. When you start to be intentional about your body movements, you can apply that to change your inner perceptions and increase self-confidence.

Scientific evidence indicates that we can enhance our self-confidence through our posture and the power of posing. So stand straight and assume the Superman pose constantly.

9. Understand what you believe and why you believe it

You can be more confident when you have carefully considered your perspectives. When you understand what you believe and why you believe it and have research to support it, it creates a high sense of confidence.

When you have solidly considered values and beliefs creates a foundation for your life and a place for everything else, you do. If that foundation is weak or vulnerable to erosion, it can affect your whole belief structure, including what you believe about yourself. This doesn't imply that you have all the solutions to life or that there is no space for mystery. Every belief can be countered to some degree.

Just know how your beliefs can be opposed, understand the arguments for and against them, and understand why you believe something even when you might not be able to prove it completely.

10. Be organized

Chaos generates uncertainty, which results to doubt. When you live a chaotic life and unorganized, it can be an environment which may not be right for high levels of self-confidence.

However, when you know where everything is and how it fits together, it generates a sense of security, which results in the self-perception that you have it under control. This is a great confidence booster.

When everything is out of control, it is hard to be confident in your abilities because it appears like a lot is up to chance. The organization builds an environment where confidence can thrive.

11. Take some risks

Taking risks and dealing with failures can be opportunities to increase your confidence. This is true when you succeed but can still work when you don't.

Why?

Because the fact that you decided to take a risk is a success in itself. Even when you failed at the task, you succeed in getting out of the comfort zone, and that can be exciting.

Consider this.

When you take a realistic risk, there are three options.

- You succeed. It is positive all around.

- You partially succeed. Positive because now you can see what you need to do to become successful.

- You fail. Partly negative and partly positive. You indeed failed, but you consider failure is important, and at the end of the day, you can be confident that you took a risk and did something to move forward.

Chapter 3: Boosting Emotional Intelligence

There are many types of intelligence, and it is our duty to find out what they are and how to combine them into our lives. Sources of intelligence can be determined in quotients. Many of us know about intelligence quotient, which is mainly related to our potential to memorize, remember things from our memory, and our logical reasoning.

There is a new curiosity quotient, which describes the ability of an individual to experience a powerful motivation to learn a specific subject.

Emotional intelligence refers to understanding your emotions and learning how to manage them. In simple terms, it involves being aware of our emotions and realizing that our emotions can determine the way we behave and impact people.

We are emotional beings who always make decisions and respond to stimuli depending on our emotions. For that reason, our strength to improve our EQ has a big impact on all of our relationships, and the way we make decisions. EQ is significantly crucial.

Here are ways that you can use to improve your emotional intelligence.

Before we look at the ways, it is important to note that the best way to boost your emotional skills is to practice in the real world. Through practice and getting a report on your performance, preferably by an experienced professional, you can change your behavior and become effective in understanding and controlling your emotions plus emotions of others.

Everyone has characteristics of their lives that they can change. While each skill discussed here can assist you in some way, you may discover some skills more crucial than others, based on your current circumstance.

1. Increase your level of self-awareness

One of the major areas of emotional intelligence is self-awareness. In many ways, this is the cornerstone of all other fields. For you to be aware of the emotions of others, you need to be aware of your own emotions first.

You can become more self-aware of your emotions by practicing different forms of meditation. By joining a group, enrolling in a course, or hiring a professional, you can employ these techniques to become more self-aware of your feelings, body, and your thoughts.

You can still become aware of your emotions by recording in a notebook your feelings at different times. By growing your emotional vocabulary and using it to describe your different feelings throughout different parts of the day, you can determine how to pay more attention to your emotions.

Besides describing your emotions, pay attention to their intensity. You can rate the emotions on a scale of 1-10. The better you can determine your emotions, the more easily you can track and change them.

2. Discover your inner passions

Everyone likes to go about their work from day-to-day. However, how many people are happy about the work they do? Many people think they are stuck in a rut at their jobs. However, no one plucked them up and plant them where they are. Normally, by the following money, people end up doing work that they currently do.

Few people work hard to do the kind of work that makes them happy. Many people have a passion to do a certain kind of work, but it is hard to realize that. You may be aware of starving artists who avoid doing regular jobs so that they can get the job of their dream. You may not be successful in finding work that you are passionate about, but with enough planning, you can succeed.

3. Show your feelings, thoughts, and beliefs

Learning how to reveal your emotions can always assist you to control your emotions. Of course, you can spoil everything and avoid sharing your real feelings, beliefs, or thoughts with anyone. However, this approach is both difficult to do, and it makes for a very lonely life. Nobody gets a chance to know you, and you don't get to know others well. All humans share the longing to have an intimate relationship with some trusted people.

On the flip side, you can decide to ramble out your innermost thoughts, beliefs, and feelings to everyone. This method can still be a mistake. First, some people don't really care about your thoughts and feelings. Secondly, others may be offended by your disclosures or see it as rude.

Aim for assertiveness. This is the correct means to share your beliefs, thoughts, and feelings. Essentially, you need to allow the right people, at the right time and know your position.

4. Understand your strengths and weaknesses

Some people think that they are excellent at everything. Others continuously undermine their strengths. The right situation is to accurately determine your strength and weaknesses. Knowing yourself allows you to make choices in life. For instance, by concentrating on your strengths you can achieve more of what you want out of life.

Going for the things you are good at and having a passion for science, public speaking, art, writing allows you to have a wealthy and fuller life. By concentrating so much on your weakness, it affects your life, and you tend to miss from getting the best out of your life.

When you need to make decisions, you may receive messages that originate from your gut. Some choices make you feel good, and others may trigger an odd feeling. You may view these feelings as messages from your heart, compared to your head. People are always guided by their emotional knowledge, which they may not entirely understand.

5. Walk in the shoes of others

Empathy is a very powerful emotion. In fact, successful leaders and politician have high empathy.

Increasing your potential to empathize can assist you to get closer to others, win their support when you require it and suppress high-charged circumstances. By revealing to the other individual that you understand where he is coming from, you develop a certain degree of respect. For instance, you show that you aren't self-centered.

Begin by being empathic by paying attention to others. Listen carefully when you communicate with someone. Listen to what she tells you and what she wants to hear. By increasing your abilities and skills to understand and pay attention to what people are trying to say, you will become more empathic.

Control the emotions of another person

If you can control the emotions of those around you, then you will have a great skill. You have perhaps come across leaders who can calm down or quiet an angry crowd. On the flip side, you have perhaps seen how certain people can misuse others emotions. Imagine the number of times a poorly prepared CEO of a company has to deal with the media in a time of crisis. By sending the wrong body language, or even avoiding responding to specific questions, these leaders make the audience to feel upset.

Controlling the emotions of others involves a two-step process. Simply follow this procedure:

1. Raise your empathy

You need to put yourself in another person's shoes and experience his or her joy, pain, fears, or hopes. One way of doing this is by asking people questions. Learn what you can manage by observing and asking. Does he prefer sports or exercise? What are his best activities and teams? What does he want to eat? What makes her feel sad or happy?

2. Respond in a manner that you would like someone to respond to you to reduce that pain.

Making someone else's emotions demands a certain level of skill. First, you need to understand where you want to direct the other individual. Do you want to make someone calm, happy, or aware? Once you decide the way you want her to feel, then you need to know how to guide her there.

Think of the last moment you listened to a motivational speaker or saw a film that moved you. Impactful experiences always require a build-up where the speaker or movie director prepares the stage where he or she demands a person to be emotionally. You develop this build-up on your own by allowing the other individual to understand where you want to go.

Next, you can develop your case using examples. You need to send to the other individual that you are both on the same boat, and it is both of your best interest to ride on the same boat. By becoming consistent in your voice, body posture, and your message, you can send out a potent message that can move the emotions of the other individual to where you want them.

6. Become socially responsible

Social responsibility is a higher degree of emotional experience. It demonstrates that you care about others, especially those who are less fortunate. Socially responsibility doesn't involve personal gain but it is about what you can do to help others.

There are different levels of social responsibility:

- At the lowest level, you can send money to charity. Although you want to donate as a part of a responsible plan, donations are the first step in the process.

- The next stage, you may help a valuable organization gather money. You can get from relatives or people you work with. You can take part in car washes, or biking events.

- The most effective elements of social responsibility are that you fight for a worthwhile reason. Consider methods that you want to start looking for the causes that you see as the most important for you. You could be passionate about providing care to the elderly, food shelters, and so on.

Once you choose a cause that you may want to support, consider how well you can help. You can volunteer, or purpose to chip in different methods.

7. Control your impulses

Controlling your emotions offers a great pillar of emotional intelligence. When you become more emotionally self-aware, you prepare yourself for emotional self-management. You can control your impulses in three ways:

- Analytic: An analytic strategy demands that you stop and analyze your thoughts when you feel impulsive. You could ask yourself questions like:
    - Could I be thinking about something different?
    - What is the best alternative thought?
    - How can thinking about this stressful situation assist me?

- Coping: This approach requires different coping thoughts that you practice early. Some of these thoughts comprise:
    - Let me think this through
    - I know I can regulate my thoughts
    - I can just slow down a bit

- I don't think of alternatives

These strategies can assist you in handling stressful challenges or events when you learn them in advance. You cannot effectively try out these approaches on the fly. With planning and practice, you can move forward in handling impulsive thoughts, actions and words.

8. Become more flexible

Virtually everybody has a routine of going about with their daily duties. For a society to run well, it demands a specific level of regulations and rules. However, there are challenges that you can experience and become inflexible.

A rigid mind will miss chances, and remain behind in learning new techniques. Becoming emotionally smart demands that you understand what to stick to and when to change your emotional connections. When the time to change comes, people with higher emotional intelligence have the upper hand.

9. Remain happy

How can you rate your level of happiness on a scale of 1-10?

People with higher emotional intelligence are always happy. And they don't just become happy because everything is going well for them.

Happiness comes from deep inside their heart. A person who knows how to control their emotions wakes up feeling happy in the morning. And when he experiences obstacles, he can still uphold a certain degree of happiness. In fact, his happiness energizes his spirit when he encounters the various challenges, and it ensures his mind remain clear, preventing him from being caught up in unproductive self-pity emotions. Happy people come up with solutions to problems compared to sad or depressed individuals.

While depressed people concentrate on details than happy people, those who are happy accomplish more than sand people. While both happiness and sadness are emotions, they always vary. So you can manage your mood to serve your own purpose. Being emotionally intelligent requires that you know when to be sad, happy, and anxious.

People like to be around people who are happy. Happy leaders have members who are highly engaged. You can find a lot of benefits to staying happy.

People will praise you more, you can overcome difficult times, you will feel better, and you will be more helpful to others. Research even indicates that happy people tend to live longer.

Very few people know how to control their happiness. People always relate happiness with material goods or with finding things from others. The really happy people are the ones that give. The people who spread happiness tend to remain happier.

Luckily, while you increase your emotional intelligence, you will still remember that it costs you nothing to spread happiness, and what you get in return is priceless.

Other strategies to enhance your emotional intelligence

1. Learn to obey your intuition

Your intuition is one of the best tools, and it should never be ignored.

For a long time, intuition and rational thinking were seen as two mutually exclusive ideas. Recently is when scientists started to understand that our intuitive emotions act as an efficient channel that enhances our potential to make better decisions.

Having this in mind, you need to learn to trust your intuition and start to depend on it more often.

2. Learn to silence your mind

When you are feeling stressed, or depressed, you lose the ability to assess a situation, hear what your friend could be saying, communicate clearly and rationally.

One skill that can enhance our emotional intelligence is to discover a means to handle stress and calm the mind during moments of emotional turmoil.

Mindfulness meditation is a vital tool for this, and applying a tool such as a Headspace app can be a great way to start.

3. Talk about your feelings

Some people relate feelings with weakness. As a result, they avoid expressing their feelings in public. However, for one to improve their emotional intelligence, it is important that you learn to show your feelings. People with high emotional intelligence aren't afraid to express their feelings. They are not scared of expressing their vulnerabilities, and feelings.

4. Understand that you are not your emotions

Many people waste most of the time thinking that they need to feel a specific way. Typically, we are raised up to believe that it is wrong to show and even experience specific emotions.

The truth is that is not the feeling that matters, but how you decide to respond to it. You aren't your emotions, and the earlier you learn to understand that, the better.

5. Practice "learned optimism"

Pay attention to how you express yourself, both good and bad. Do you take credit for your efforts or assume it is pure luck?

Do you take control of your missed steps or does it look normal to divert the blame on something different? Learn to be optimistic and create space in your emotional and spiritual life.

6. Begin with your ego

Ego plays a big role in the way you perceive different situations. You cannot feel unappreciated unless you let yourself feel that way. And since you are feeling that way implies that your ego has been damaged. But you need to remember that you aren't your ego. You are a spiritual being who is supposed to remain happy, and not resent anything.

7. Think about how you think

You may not always determine the people or situation you work with, but you can always determine how you develop it in your mind. Spend a lot of time thinking about how you respond to situations and why. This will deliver clarity you need to begin selecting new patterns.

8. Choose your words wisely

The words we use have emotional weight and trigger specific connections in the mind. One method of changing your thoughts and acquiring negative emotions under control is to choose positive words and become more concerned about your speech.

9. Step into their shoes

Being able to understand a given situation from another person's perspective is an ability that most of us acquire at the age of 5.

In some environments, we are overcome by negative emotions and begin to act as if we are 4, appreciating our emotions, and arguments.

The next time you are in the middle of a heated argument, you need to try and step into another person's shoes to understand where they are coming from.

You may discover that they have a great point. Regardless of this, this method will improve your understanding of the other person.

.

10. Release anger out

Anger is a powerful emotion that has "side-effects." Once your anger disappears, you start to feel drained and stupid. One way that you can control your anger is to avoid things that may irritate you. Take a few deep breaths, let your breath drive the anger and tension, and allow you to relieve your mind.

11. Show yourself some love

If you do a given action well-then you need to celebrate. Learn from the experience and improve the next time. There is no point of pulling yourself behind for every small mistake. Criticizing and judging yourself will not make you better. On the other hand, understanding, compassion, and self-awareness will.

12. Give yourself some positive feedback

Train yourself to see things that are worth to complement instead of concentrating on little things that can be judged in others. When you learn to compliment and avoid judging, your EQ will increase and your relationship will improve.

13. Choose your battles

Arguments consume time and energy, in particular, if you want to correct them in a positive note. Before you get yourself into one, take time to think of what is worth to argue about and what is best left alone.

14. Know your buttons

Pay attention to the moments when you allow others to push your buttons. What are your stimulators? What are the right conditions that are likely to let your guard down?

Try to avoid getting into circumstances which you aren't able to select a graceful response.

15. Identify people's nonverbal communication

The secret to successful relationships at work and harmony in your family depends on your potential to understand non-verbal cues channeled through body language and gestures. Having the ability to read these cues allows you to become empathetic and improve your relationships.

16. Search for sarcasm

Sarcasm is always a sign that an individual is defensive. When you hear sarcasm or you are the one using it, then you need to ask yourself why? What is the hidden emotion? Why are you or the other individual being defensive?

17. Practice social responsibility

Today there is an increasing desire, and demand for more social responsibility in the work settings, especially from customers and employers. Studies indicate that social responsibility is a retention advantage, especially among the younger generations. Workers reward socially responsible companies and organizations with an increased level of participation, which results in increased revenue and productivity.

However, it doesn't end there. More and more social responsibility is required at every individual level. Although it is not fully identified by many, it is a primary field of emotional intelligence. Social responsibility is the biggest level of emotional experience.

It demonstrates that you are concerned about others, in particular, the less fortunate. Being socially responsible is what you contribute to help others.

SR demands that you do your duty to help the environment, volunteering your time to those in need, and being courteous in all you carry out.

- SR means to be motivated internally to act in a compassionate way.
- Being socially responsible isn't about personal interest. It involves what you contribute to assist other people.
- SR is supporting a proactive position towards positively affecting the people and environments around you.

Tips and Exercises

- If you have a choice to pick two products and one product provides a good cause or was created in an ethical manner, then buy that product.
- You can start to volunteer once a month in a place that suits your interests and skills.
- In the workplace, look for opportunities to help your workgroup. If you discover that a team member seems to be behind their work, you can offer to help instead of saying that is not your job.

It is only through the dedication to embrace and uphold social responsibility into your personal value and belief system can you become socially responsible in everything you do. The last point to look at social responsibility is to become part of the solution instead of the problem.

18. Spending time to reflect

To interact with emotions problems, demand inner work-personal reflection time. Time provides you space to reflect on your feelings and emotions so that you can understand them. It offers you space to sort out and express your thoughts and emotions. Life can be challenging. When we apply reflection as a tool, we are able to stand back objectively and review our lives and what we deal with. It is also the strength to reflect on the "here and now," on your thoughts and feelings. This also involves reflecting on emotions, thoughts and the feelings of others. Reflection still allows us to learn more about ourselves so that we can move on to make better choices.

Without ever meditating, we are likely to concentrate on how many times we have failed instead of look at how much we have been successful at. When the day ends, set aside 30 minutes to meditate on the various emotions you encountered during the day. Note them down. Now comes the challenging part. What actions followed it? Was it right? How can you respond effectively the next time?

Tips and exercise

Exercise: A great time to reflect is when you are at the gym. You can use this time to think about your life and work. For some people, the best ideas arise during the "gym time." If you don't go to the gym, try to run or take in part in another daily exercise, think of taking a walk and using that moment for reflection.

Journaling: Journaling is a great wat to record thoughts while they take place. Writing your thoughts down allows you to handle challenges as they occur. But the biggest advantage is that it provides you time to reflect. Self-reflection is the secret to changing how you feel and how you persevere. Physically writing things down causes you to concentrate on what is important.

Writing can happen daily or only when you think you need to express yourself. Many people like to set aside a fixed time of day, before being prepared for bed. But you basically need to do it, there is no right or wrong way. Keep in mind that revealing your emotions in your journal can be an important outlet for relieving stress, so you should attempt to write about your hopes, thoughts, frustrations, and fears, and any other emotions you are experiencing.

Here is a recommendation for handling frustration. Stop and review. The best things you can do is to mentally stop yourself, and meditate on the circumstance. Find out why you feel frustrated.

Note it down, and be specific. Try to remember a positive thing about your present situation. For example, if your boss is late for your meeting, then you have additional time to prepare. Or you could use this time to relax a bit.

Other methods to reflect include setting aside time for yourself on a daily basis, even if it is just a few minutes every day.

Here are more suggestions:

- Write- we all have something interesting to tell
- A cup of tea outside or in your bed can be relaxing.
- Stretch, or take a walk
- Read a book that interests you.
- Draw or paint

The more you meditate the better you will become.

Chapter 4: Self-Confidence

By definition, self-esteem is the value you give yourself. An individual with self-confidence knows that they can overcome any obstacles that they face regardless of how difficult it can be. They know that they can do something, and believe that they can do it well.

However, this does not mean that a self-confident individual will never feel nervous because these are natural emotions which we all go through. Instead, it implies that a self-confident individual can persevere regardless of these emotions, and this is what makes them achieve their goals.

Some of the characteristics of a self-confident individual include:

- Breathes naturally and easily
- Works towards goals with an expectation of success instead of failure.
- Can laugh at themselves and accept constructive criticism
- Feels like in the end things will be fine regardless of what
- Believe that they can handle the challenges that lie ahead of them.

As you can see, there is no magic in becoming self-confident. Self-confident individuals believe in their abilities and themselves. Therefore, this belief allows them to concentrate on what they need and then look for it in the best way they know.

The more self-confident you become, the higher your concentration will be. According to the law of attraction, this will lead to acquiring more of what you want and less of what you don't want.

It is critical to remember that confidence is rarely corrected at a certain degree. Instead, it is typical for an individual's self-confidence to change from day-to-day or even month to month.

For instance, you could be experiencing a bad day today because you didn't achieve what you wanted. For that reason, your confidence has experienced some damages, and it is lower than usual.

On the other hand, you might be having a great day where everything is going well just as you had arranged. Naturally, under the following conditions, your self-confidence is going to increase.

So when considering your current state of confidence, don't look at it in a short time frame like a few hours a day, that is not an accurate representation of how confident you are. However, you need to try to consider the average level of confidence over the past month.

For instance:

- Have you been in a bad mood and you were afraid to begin a new project because you felt like you would fail at them?
- Have you been highly on a great mood and you were unable to attain the goals which you set for yourself?

Once you have decided your average level of confidence, you can proceed to apply that estimation as the measure of the amount of progress you make to improve your confidence level.

What determines how confident you are?

While there are many aspects which determine how confident an individual feel, all confident people share a certain characteristic and trait.

To assist you have a better understanding of what these are, you can attempt to answer the following questions:

1. Where are you heading in life?

For one to be happy in life, they must know where they are heading.

Do you know where you are heading and what you want to be in life?
Individuals who don't know where they are heading lack self-confidence because they feel their life has no real direction to it. They feel that they will always remain where they are and become so depressed about their life circumstance.

2. What motivates you?

The things that motivate you will make you feel great about yourself and fill you with enough energy required to achieve your goals.

Consider the things that you do in the whole day. Do they excite you? Do they increase your attention?

If you don't feel motivated in life, then you are unlikely to perform things which will increase your level of confidence.

3. Can you regulate your emotions?

If you cannot control your emotions, they will end up taking charge of your life.

Are you an individual who can control your emotions and respond properly to them? Or you can let them control you, and finally, regret?

Individuals who cannot control their emotions are guided by them, and so they often end up missing on many opportunities that could have increased their confidence.

4. What is your level of positivity?

The way you decide to perceive things determines how you will respond to them?

Are you a positive person who is hopeful for the future? Or are you always sad with a pessimistic attitude?

People that don't have a positive mindset are likely to doubt their ability to do something, which then makes them never start or give up halfway through.

But you need to be careful with this, because individuals who concentrate on the positive and don't want to listen to anything negative, have a habit of denying the truth. This means they see only what they want to see.

5. How do you look at yourself?

When you lack self-acceptance, it leads to self-rejection, which means you will never have self-confidence.

When you are self-aware, it means you know how you look like to other people. Self-awareness is also connected to self-acceptance, which is the level in which you can accept your image.

People who are unable to accept themselves are self-rejecting. This mindset can generate a higher degree of self-confidence.

6. How flexible are you?

Can you change your behavior and opinions based on the situation you experience or information that is delivered? Or do you have a rigid mindset concerning how thing need to be and you are unwilling to change those beliefs?

If you aren't ready to change your views and accept, then what you currently consider as real may be false, additionally, you will find it difficult in life to change yourself for the better.

Self-confidence develops through experience. Therefore, if you always believe that what you are doing is right, there is nothing that you will learn, and your confidence will never increase.

7. Do you challenge yourself?

Do you enjoy to learn new things and challenge your mindset? Or do you like to remain in your comfort zone, and continue to do the same things over and over again?

Personal growth happens when you step outside of your comfort zone. The longer you refuse to make that extra step, the more difficult it would be to increase your confidence.

8. How do you treat your body?

How you feel in the whole day is determined by the chemicals and hormone moving around your body. If you take junk food and do not exercise, then your body will suffer, and so your confidence will be affected.

Therefore, if you are working on your mind, you must also improve your body. If you fail to do so, it will lead to slow or non-existent change.

9. Can you take risks

If you aren't sure about how something is going to be, do you take a risk? Or do you opt to play it safe?

People who are ready to take risks in life learn to build confidence quickly, because they are stepping out into the unknown when most individuals would have stepped back.

If the risk is great, then their confidence is likely to increase. However, when the risk doesn't pay off, their confidence may take a different turn, but they will still have a feeling of satisfaction that they at least made an effort to try.

Risks are something that you need to take to grow as an individual, and they are also one of the best methods to step outside your comfort zone.

But keep in mind, don't take risks just for the sake of it. Take calculated risks that you think has some opportunity of paying off. If they don't, try something else until you succeed.

10. What is the purpose of your life?

What are you currently doing? What do you want to do?

Individuals who feel that their actions have a purpose are likely to have a higher level of confidence than people who see their efforts as meaningless.

When you have a sense of purpose concerning your life, it is the most critical things that you can discover, but it can also be the most difficult.

Characteristics of individuals with low self-esteem and how to boost your low self-esteem

- **Do you neglect yourself?**

If you have a low self –esteem, most likely you don't take care of yourself. You could be seeing self-care as a waste of time, or you could be thinking you aren't worth to take care of yourself.

- **Do you doubt yourself?**

If you doubt yourself, it means you have a conflicting perception of yourself. Most times, this conflicting thought becomes negative self-talk, and it builds a negative self-image.

No matter how wise or knowledgeable an individual is, this person cannot be perfect all the time. We all make mistakes. Making mistakes is a fundamental part of achieving your goal of being successful.

Collect all the information you require on the subject you have to take a decision on and decide.

Yes, it will happen; sometimes, you may not make the best decision. However, it is better to make any decision instead of none.

Are you an expert at doubting yourself? If you are, then you need to begin now to use this skill to doubt things on the following list.

Start doubting that:

- Skilled enough
- Good enough
- Liked, loved, and appreciated
- Beautiful enough

Here are the things you need to know that you should begin doubting yourself. These things are the negative things that you are saying to yourself.

I don't mean you change your mind right away. For now, begin doubting yourself.

Start doubting and provide yourself an opportunity to discover who you are.

- **Do you have low self-esteem?**

Both self-esteem and self-confidence are connected.

If you have one, probably you have the other one as well. If one is low, then the other one is likely low.

Both self-esteem and self-confidence are important, and both define the kind of individual you are.

Self-esteem is about who you believe you are, and self-confidence is what you believe you can do.

The challenging part of having low self-confidence is that you need to demonstrate your strength before you can enhance your self-confidence.

You cannot be confident about a specific ability before you do it.

Your success gives you the self-confidence to do it again, or attempt similar things.

But you need to realize that self-confidence isn't a continuum.

Depending on the task, or your goal, your self-confidence will rise from high to low and the other way around.

This change is normal, and once you improve your self-esteem, you will be more than able to handle this fluctuation in a manner that doesn't negatively affect your success but assists you to improve your capabilities more and more.

Many individuals believe that they aren't confident enough. And most people consider having high self-confidence critical to realize their dreams, get their result, or even set goals in the first place.

Self-confidence isn't a continuum because it relies on more than one element. But we are doing well to remain less confident sometimes.

Some "lucky" ones have no problems in life, no obstacles, and no pains. The rest of us, we are having them all. All the things to solve, and all the situations to face and so on.

All of this problem that you encounter, you pass it sooner or later. So you know how you can handle everything else. It makes sense, right?

The past is the best predictor of the future, and the past indicates how you will emerge from any situation you will face.

Anytime you doubt yourself, consider all the difficult circumstances that you encounter.

Keep in mind, the only confidence you need as a continuum is this one:

Whatever comes your way, you will find the means to deal with it.

For certain reasons, self-confidence will emerge from the successes you will experience. You cannot probably be self-confident about your driving before you learn how to drive, right? Those who are self-confident about their driving skills before learning to drive are a risk to society.

You cannot be confident about mastering something before you create several examples that you can do it.

You can be confident, like the way you have been in the past, you can learn any skill and become a master at it.

If you motivate yourself about the time when your self-confidence is low, low will remain because you will not provide yourself with the opportunity to prove yourself how great you can be, how many important things you can achieve.

- **Are you afraid to put yourself first?**

Sometimes it could be that you don't put yourself first because you believe that a person needs your attention urgently. Other times you don't put yourself first because becoming altruistic generates positive feelings.

What about the moments when you don't put yourself first?

If you have low self-esteem, maybe you put others first even though you may feel:

- You could feel bad about it.
- You feel bad about yourself.
- You feel like the real you disappearing whenever you deny yourself the right to put yourself first.

Yes, there are times when it is a good thing to put others first.

But this happens every day and in almost every situation. Most likely, you are doing it out of fear or anxiety.

You may have the fear that you will not be loved, liked, or seen as a good person, and so on.

The result of putting others first all the time will not generate your love, nor acceptance, nor will you be liked more.

The outcome will be that you get tired. You could develop a resentment towards the people you always prioritize, and from here, there are just a few steps to destroy a great relationship.

Typically, if you prioritize others first because of low self-esteem, most probably those people will not ask you to put them first or sacrifice yourself for them. Thus, they will appreciate your effort, and they will not be thankful for it.

So what do you need to do?

Putting yourself first doesn't mean that you are selfish or self-centered.

It is a different thing to wake up with the idea of: "What can I do today for my spouse?" and a different thing to do nothing all day but fulfill the needs of your spouse ignoring your needs.

- **Are you afraid to trust your ideas, judgment, and opinion?**

Trusting your judgment, ideas, and opinions begins by letting yourself to feel and move with the feeling you have.

Respecting your opinions, and judgment is a matter of deciding instead of lacking self-esteem. But it becomes a challenge when you beat yourself about it.

Nearly everything that you beat yourself about will finally become a self-esteem challenge because you avoid giving yourself a chance.

- To bring out the best in you
- To do your best
- To prove yourself how great and capable you are.

- Do you accentuate your negative points?

All humans have a good side, and not too good as well.

Self-esteem is the result of your mind. Enhancing your negative points will generate low self-esteem because where your attention runs to, your energy runs as well. Plus, your unconscious mind doesn't let you become a liar.

This implies that your mind will do its best to demonstrate that you are correct, good and bad doesn't matter because you are right, as long as you tell the truth.

If you choose to pay attention to the negative side of yourself, you will probably garnish this picture with comprehensive and hurtful self-talk.

And your mind will do the best to prove every statement that you make about yourself.

- **Are you too concerned about what people might say about you?**

Human beings are social. This means we care about what people think about us, and to some extent, we need to care if we want to belong.

Probably you know that regardless of how hard you try, you will never satisfy everyone. Some people like mangoes and others like apples. Regardless of what you will do to mango, the apple lovers will continue to love apples, and vice versa.

But the harder you try to satisfy everybody, the fewer people will be satisfied with you.

Getting concerned about what people may think of you originates from too much thinking, a lot of analysis of how you behave, or how people react to different circumstances. If the response is negative, a lot of thinking may make you conclude that it was your fault in some way.

People will think about you whatever they want to think of you and sometimes what people think of you has nothing to do with you, with the person you have, but has everything to do with who they are.

What people may say about you is subjective and shouldn't be the measure of your behavior or your feelings about self.

Your morals and values should be the basis of your actions and behavior because the kind of person you need to satisfy the most is yourself.

Let your morals and values to direct you. They already have the correct measure of caring you deserve to be a great person, and the person you want to become.

You cannot dictate what people say or think about you. However, you can change the way you behave and how you respond to the behaviors of others.

As long as you do the best, you know, it should be sufficient for everybody around you. Those who aren't comfortable with that, don't deserve your effort and attention.

- **Do you reward yourself for the accomplishments you make?**

It might be difficult to reward yourself for the achievements you have made because:

- You could think that it is a small achievement to be realized.
- You could ignore the effort you have put in.
- You may think that your achievement is because of somebody else.
- You may tend to stress what you don't achieve, and by doing so, your achievements may appear too small.
- You might consider achieving your accomplishments as evidence of having a big negative ego.

Rewarding yourself for the achievements you have attained is a means of reinforcing positive actions.

It is not about vanity but creating a map for yourself.

- A map that will save you energy and time.
- A map that will allow you to remain focused on your goals.
- A map that will assist you in your journeys towards what you want and require a desire.

- **Do you accept compliments**

Some of the things that may prevent you from accepting accomplishments when you have low self-esteem:

- You consider the achievements that you are complimented for, to others.
- What you think about yourself doesn't match what other people say about yourself.

- You fear that if you accept the compliment, it means that the next time you will need to do it even better.
- You don't trust that you deserve a compliment.
- You believe that you are complimented because the other person understands how bad you are, and they are complimenting you to make you feel better.

How you should not accept a compliment

Avoid saying that it was nothing.

Besides putting the effort to achieve something, you could be perceived as arrogant.

Don't respond with several examples you haven't been doing great.

Also, don't put yourself down and then complete the smearing with 100 reasons why you should stay there.

- **Are you mean to yourself but kind to others?**

The good and kind to others arises from your values, and morals, plus the need to work together.

But it comes from a strong motive to be liked and accepted. Regardless of your self-esteem level, you want to be like, don't you? You want to be considered as a great person. You want to create a positive image in the eyes of people close to you.

Do you believe that being nice and good to others leads to being accepted and loved?

If yes, imagine giving yourself the same treatment.

Do you know that if you begin to treat yourself as good the way you treat others, you will attain the same result with yourself? You acknowledge yourself you are; you love yourself the way you are.

- **Do you have a negative internal dialog?**

How do you end up feeling low?
The first thing is a negative internal dialog.
We all experience "dead" moments throughout the day.
Times like:

- Waiting inline
- Any other waiting time.
- I am waiting for the bus.

You can start to change your thoughts and become positive using these dead moments.

Every time you have to wait for something, take your thoughts seriously towards the positive things that surround you.

It doesn't have to be something out of the ordinary.

- It can be the color of a moving vehicle.
- It can be a person smiling.
- It can be a beautiful pink in a girl's hair.
- It can be the architecture of a building.

Look for the beauty around you, and you will be surprised by the number of things you have missed in the past.

Allow yourself to enjoy big things around you, and your mind will reward you with happiness and positive thoughts.

You will only recognize and see things you are looking for.

If you tend to search for your negative points, only that is what you will get because you lack the awareness that you have positive aspects as well. You become blind to them.

Your mind is operating like Google or Amazon.

If you search for a topic on Google, Google will begin to show you the subject you have looked for. The more you click on that topic, the more connected things with that subject Google displays.

12 powerful tips to improve your self-esteem

Nobody can go back and start again beginning, but anyone can start today and create a new ending.

Having a high opinion about yourself, and who you are and what you do and loving yourself is one of the things that people always miss, or have too little of in the current society.

Discovering your confident self

Now that you know some of the things that can make a person confident, how much of what you have learned do you think works for you?

Keep in mind each of these characteristics will allow you to grow your self-confidence.

Therefore, your first step is to decide what traits you think you have and then to decide what you need to work on. These areas need to be enhanced slowly but don't expect to master them overnight.

If you can achieve everything discussed on this list, you will become a very confident individual who can comfortably handle the challenges that life throws.

Your thoughts and beliefs

The main causes of low self-confidence include the thoughts that you have daily, especially the ideas which are self-defeating.

These kinds of thoughts will slow you down and decrease your self-worth and self-esteem. Therefore, you end up feeling worse about yourself, which then affects your self-confidence.

Some of the common self-defeating thoughts start with terms such as:

- "I will always be…."
- "I can't do that…."
- "There is no way that I could…"
- "….is impossible."

These phrases are just some of the many types of negative self-talk that individuals use daily. They are signs of self-rejecting mind and a condition of low confidence.

A self-rejecting mind

This is the mind that opposes itself. In other words, this mind is limited by self-imposed limitations.

Some of the restrictions are beliefs that a person has acquired from society, parents, and now guide their actions and thoughts.

However, most of the restricting beliefs are not real. They have no basis in reality. They are false statements, and misconceptions about yourself, and the world that you live.

When something challenges your limiting beliefs, it changes the way you look at reality.

Limiting beliefs will destroy the truth and prevent you from seeing the truth about yourself and the environment you live in.

You will start to see a version of reality which you are restricted because of certain disadvantages which you believe you have. This causes you to live your life within those restrictions, and never experience the full version of reality that surrounds you.

This is achieved by realizing your strengths, and using those strengths to become a better person. Let us look at some ways that you can realize this:

Identify your strengths

In general, you will realize that the things which you are good at, and which you consider as important to you will be parts of your life that your self-confidence is at its highest.

Equally, if you aren't good at something critical to you, then your self-confidence is likely to be lower.

What this means is that your self-confidence originates from your strengths and your values. This means self-esteem emerges from the things which you are an expert and think are important.

So the first thing that a person should do to boost their levels of confidence is, to begin with, their strengths.

By doing so, they will manage to grow an existing foundation of confidence. All that is required is to continue growing your confidence until it attains a level that you are satisfied with.

This is realized by accepting the things which you are currently good at and accepting praise from others for the things you do great.

Once you begin to respect yourself for your talents, that self-respect will slowly spread to other parts of your life, allowing you to gain confidence in other things.

To assist you in choosing what you are good at, try to consider things that you have done well at school, home, or work, and then consider any future actions which you could do to grow those talents.

For instance, if you think making people laugh is one of your greatest talents because people laugh at the jokes you crack, then you may choose to grow that talent by reading humor psychology books.

Therefore, the basic template is:

- What are you good at.

- An instance of when you did it well.

- How can I grow this talent?

Once you are done with this process, you need to know what you are good at and understand the things that you can do to begin growing your self-confidence.

Ask others what you are good at

If you still don't know what you are good at, then you can decide to ask your friends. Assume that the things which we are good at others are also good at, and thus discount them even if they are perfectly valid talents.

Here are some questions that you can ask others to determine what you are most talented at:

- What could I do less of?

- What do you think I am good at?

- How do you think I could enhance my skills?

- What could I do more of?

The basis of these questions is to develop an idea of the things that you are good at, why you are good at them and how you can grow them. Once you identify your talents, you will have something to work on and increase your self-confidence.

Unveiling unknown talents

One of the advantages of asking others what your talents are, aside from just deciding on your own, is that we see ourselves differently to how others see us.

For instance, we can do things which are unaware of, or we could be doing things the wrong way and still fail to know. So telling others about ourselves can help us to see things which we didn't see before.

Additionally, when you speak to different people, you will be able to identify patterns in the responses that you get. So when you discover that everyone is saying the same thing about you, then it would be good to proceed to implement what they are saying.

Similarly, if you ask five people to give their feedback and only one person says something negative about you, then you may need to ignore what they have said or ask a different person if they agree or not.

This process will allow you to better understand yourself, and the process of learning that other people believe you are talented will boost your self-esteem to a higher level than it is currently is.

It is all about you

People that have no self-confidence and self-esteem consider the needs of others before their own. One reason why they do this is that they want to be accepted by others. So they believe that the more they sacrifice their needs, the more they will be liked and accepted.

When you begin to become more self-confident, you will realize that the reverse is true. Rather than think about what other people want, you begin to think more about what you want.

Some people think that this can make you a very selfish individual.

However, being selfish doesn't mean you are a bad person. Selfishness can help a person achieve what they want in life and make you care for those who are close to you.

If you are not selfish, the reverse will happen. You will not get what you want in life, and people will take advantage of your life. Thus, if you don't put yourself first, you will always come second.

This means that you deserve less than others, a belief which will be sent to your subconscious where it will then affect your action and thoughts.

So it is clear that considering others before yourself is not something that will boost your self-esteem or your self-confidence. This is why you must remove this belief that prioritizing yourself first is bad.

If selfish is still a problem for you, then you should assess how being unselfish has helped you so far. Of course not well, and that is why you need to be selfish.

From today start by putting your needs first, if you don't do this, you will not manage to improve your self-confidence.

The need for responsibility

When something doesn't go well in your life, what do you resort to? If you are like many people, you look for something to direct the blame, because by doing so you feel better.

When it comes to boosting your self-confidence, blaming someone or something else is what you want to avoid because once you pass the blame on someone or something, you are changing your control to other things or people.

What this means is that instead of controlling your life, you let other people control it for you. Of course, this makes you powerless to change the things for better. How can you hope to improve something which you lack personal control?

For that reason, self-confidence requires that you become responsible for your actions, and this includes both things that go wrong and right.

If you can accept to take responsibility for how your life goes, you will increase your self-confidence.

A person who fails to take charge of their actions when something wrong happens, will feel sorry for themselves or even blame others.

They think that they are a victim, and because they feel like a victim, they feel powerless to make their life take a new direction.

As you may imagine, having this mentality is not going to help a person increase their level of self-confidence or self-esteem because without accepting self-responsibility, these are things that they consider to be beyond their control.

That is why it is important to keep in mind that how a person feels happy with their life, is directly proportional to the level of control they feel they have over it. The less control you have, the worse you will feel. The more control you have, the better you will feel.

Blamer mindset

A blamer is an individual who cannot accept personal responsibility for the way things have happened. They are considered by others as individuals who like to complain, create excuses, and have a negative perception about life.

Ask yourself whether you would like to be friends with this person, or hang out? You wouldn't, and neither would anyone else, which is the reason why blamers only attract negative people into their life instead of positive people.

The effect of this can be dangerous one's level of self-confidence and self-esteem because people tend to be like the people they spend the most time with.

So in case all an individual does is spend time with negative people, then they are likely to spend all their life locked in a mindset of blame and victimhood instead of trying to look for methods to make things better for themselves.

If you want to be positive, and hang around positive people, then complaining all the time isn't going to bring them close to you. But it will attract the wrong kind of people in your life, the kind of people who will make it difficult, for you to change things and increase your self-confidence.

Learning through life experiences

The experiences that you go through in life change the kind of person you become. As a result, the person you are today occurs as a direct result of your past experiences, and so the kind of person you become will happen as a result of your future experiences.

Overall, there are two kinds of experiences you can go through include positive experiences and negative experiences.

Learning from negative life experiences

While no one likes to go through negative experiences, they can be more valuable to your personal growth than good experiences all the time.

But since they are unpleasant to handle, many people try to forget about them or blame others.

If you want to start to raise your level of self-confidence, then you need to embrace negative experiences. This includes those that have happened to you in the past and those that will happen to you in the future.

Embracing positive experiences means acknowledging them, and realizing that in some situations, you are responsible for the way something happens.

When you can accept the bad things that happen in your life, then you will be able to learn from them, and use those experiences to make yourself stronger.

If you can use this mentality of learning from your mistakes, you will find that it is easy to handle negative experiences and thus gain more control over your life.

Handling negative experiences

Some life situations will be more painful, and difficult to accept than others, and these while they are the hardest to overcome, will be the kind of experiences that provide you the best ability to improve your self-confidence.

For instance, you will experience a lot of pain if a relationship with an individual you loved ends. This is perfectly natural because painful experiences are painful for a reason; they make us feel pain. But for every bad thing that takes place, something positive will happen. You may be wondering why it always happens this way, but it could be because of the law of the universe.

Creating new life experiences

Since our life experiences define the type of individual we become, if you only experience the same things in your life, then you will not change much as an individual. By experiencing new things, you provide yourself the best opportunity to become a better individual.

The reason for this is that every experience you go through in life builds a belief in your mind. These beliefs resemble computer programs in the sense that they make you act in one way or another by affecting the kind of thoughts you experience.

Therefore, if you have a negative experience, a belief connected to that experience will be developed, which will then continue to affect you throughout your whole life.

The secret is to replace that bad experience with a good experience so that you can delete that belief and replace it with a good one.

For instance, if you were bullied at school, and you never stood up for yourself, that will develop a belief in your mind that will continue to lower your confidence as you grow older.

But if you can do something to remove that belief like learning to defend yourself, becoming fit and healthy, then you will eliminate the negative influence of that belief, and your self-confidence will increase.

This example is common among boxers.

So you need to learn to face the things we fear and start to do something about it to change the way it makes us feel. It is through this action that we empower ourselves with the ability to increase our self-confidence.

Visualize confidence

When you think about a confident person, you perhaps assume that you are confident in all spheres of life. However, even the most confident people have fears which they would rather live without.

A great example of this can be with beautiful people. Most people like to think of attractive people as being very confident and not having much that they hate about themselves.

However, the reality is that attractive individuals have a lot of insecurities regarding their appearance, and so many are not as confident as they seem.

What this shows us about self-confidence is that perception plays a big role in the way we see people. If a person appears confident to us, then we will assume that they are confident people. Therefore, the way we react towards them will be different from how we handle a person who seemed to lack self-confidence.

So if you don't have a lot of self-confidence now, it is possible to project the appearance of high self-confidence by displaying a confident body language.

With sufficient time, this new pattern of behavior will begin to imprint itself on your mind, and before you realize it, you will start to behave in a more confident way automatically. This means you have to fake it until you make it.

The most important, this procedure will happen entirely by itself because of the automatic state of human behavior. It has been revealed, for instance, that the more times you carry out a task, the better you become at it.

Finally, you reach a stage where you no longer have to think about how you will consciously implement that task, as you will eventually manage to do it with little thoughts.

However, you will require to become careful so that it doesn't work against you. In other words, if you behave in a manner that shows you don't have confidence, then the lack of confidence will result in less self-confidence.

Keep in mind that to fake something, you will require to have a clear picture of what you want to be. A great picture of exactly what confidence implies to you. One of the best ways to realize this is by using the power of mental visualization.

Visualization exercise

Here is a simple exercise you can do to improve your self-confidence:

Imagine yourself as a highly confident person and then use that image to an actual future event. Try to discover the things that you are doing, the people that you are with, the talents, and skills you have, and how you are feeling. This image of yourself should be the right person that you would like to become.

Although you will not attain your visualized image the first time you do it in real life, you will slowly but automatically begin to incorporate that image into your personality the more you visualize the super confident new you.

Visualization works because a lot of studies have demonstrated that when you imagine something in your head, it triggers the same parts of the brain as if you were doing the things you are imagining. In other words, visualizing something is like doing the same thing in real life.

However, you mustn't depend upon visualization alone. This is because to create a change in your life, both mental and physical activity is required.

Therefore, every night before you go to sleep, spend some minutes to think about the ideal you. The person that you know you can be.

If you are sensible about this visualization, your subconscious will begin to work automatically to ensure that mental image becomes a reality.

Displaying confident body language

The first thing that a person sees is your body. And so, it is the first thing that people use to measure their level of self-confidence. For that reason, if an individual wants to display confidence to others, they have to reveal the body language of a confident individual.

Some of the methods that a person can signal confidence using body language are described below:

1. Standing up straight

Maintaining a straight back shows that you are confident and alert. Individuals who slouch are generally considered as being lazy and lack confidence.

2. Smile

If you feel good about yourself on the inside, you will naturally smile. When others see this smile, they will consider you as a confident individual.

People that never smile are generally said to be miserable, and when you are miserable, individuals try to stay away from you.

3. Make eye contact

A confident individual can stare at someone directly in their eyes. People who cannot maintain eye contact tend to be weak and untrustworthy.

4. Close body proximity

Leaning forward or getting closer to another individual is a means of displaying confidence. You are showing that you aren't intimidated by their presence, and you feel comfortable in your skin.

5. Strong handshake

A strong handshake is an excellent way to reveal that you are a strong and confident individual who is not pushed over. Individuals with limp handshakes are regarded as submissive or weak.

Chapter 5: The Power of Neurolinguistics Program

Neuro-linguistic programming is a method to self-improvement and personal development that depends on the concept that successful characteristics can be brought through structuring and the underlying thought patterns and interpersonal communications.

How does it work

The different explanations of NLP make it difficult to define it. It is based on people work by internal "maps" of the world that they learn through sensory.

NLP attempts to change unconscious biases or limitations of an individual world.

NLP isn't hypnotherapy. But it works through the conscious application of language to create change in thoughts and behavior.

For instance, a major feature of NLP is the concept that an individual prefers one system.

Therapists can realize this preference via language.

An NLP expert will search for a person's PRS and use their therapeutic framework. This framework may require building rapport, setting goals, and information-gathering.

Effective mind control techniques tip in NLP

The methods used to control the mind of others is an amazing type of destructing power that exists in society. The mind is more responsive in paying attention to activities in the external world.

Some are recognized, and the rest are just skipped. However, these pieces of information are mainly processed by the brain. We get 100s of information in a second using our five senses — both our conscious and subconscious mind filters this data.

This filtering relies on specific conditions. And this made it weaker to these powers where it is an important tool to regulate the thoughts of a person.

The mind control methods can affect one's proceeding actions because these measures are the outcome of the thoughts in your mind initially regulated. These methods depend on Neuro-Linguistic Programming that can regulate the mind of people using effective patterns.

Regulating thoughts

The activities of the mind can be reviewed using EEG, and this reveals the state of one's consciousness, alertness, and the intensity of the thought.

The baseline is the beta state using higher frequencies of the mind with the constant collision of thought waves. Mental frequencies are also said to be greater than the beta state.

After the beta state, there is the alpha state with a lower rate where the mind becomes calm with decreased thought waves. This condition is one of the most critical states of the mind in psychology,

The classical hypnosis relied on the process of subjecting the individuals in the alpha state so that their mind becomes more suggestive to the commands and can be enhanced. But the NLP techniques can induce the thoughts in the target's unconscious mind.

The persuasive spirit is high in neuro-linguistic programming, and this approach is applied in the politics, business, and socializing.

While the state of mental frequencies of the alpha or theta state of meditation is similar, they differ in their characteristics. Alpha is the first phase of meditation, and it will be upgraded to an advanced level with a modified state of consciousness.

A 30-minute meditation can generate the effect of six hours sleep by activating the chemicals linked to sleep, but a sleep of six hours does not generate the benefits of a 30-minute meditation.

The perception of the mind

The perception of the surrounding reveals an unconscious influence on one's thoughts to a specific degree. About 99 percent of our cognitive activity can be nonconscious.

This means it is possible to deceive a person's mind by putting an object or anything in the vicinity of the subject that overcomes the conscious mind which is acquired by the subconscious mind.

Several tactics of the mentalist employ this principle as they may put on a red tie that will be ignored by the conscious mind, and directed to the subconscious mind of the observer applying specific methods.

These thoughts are induced in the observer in an organized way that is applied by expert NLP professionals. The point is that the subtler the suggestions are, the more subconscious the mind gets affected.

The restrictions of mind go past our perception. It can be made to perform amazing stuff.

Mind control methods

Here are some of the best mind control techniques applied by NLP experts to control others mind.

1. Being attentive to the person

The experts pay attention to the cues of a person such as a pupil dilation, body language, eye movements, and breathing. They can interpret the state of mind of an individual because the immediate emotion of an individual is the link of such cues. These eye movements can be identified to analyze how an individual perceive and process information. For example, if one subject was requested about the color of his car, and he responded with his eyes moving to the right, it will be a visual recall of the color of the car.

2. Speaking with a suggestive human mind frequency

Speaking words close to the beats of the human heart. For example, 45-72 beats per minute, that is enough to activate the higher state of suggestibility to the mind.

3. Secretly establishing the rapport easily

The expert NLP professionals employ vicious language to improve suggestibility. The connection with you will be developed closely by examining you, and subtly pretending your body language, making you weaker to their recommendations.

4. Overcoming the conscious mind using Voice roll

This approach is the process of the voice roll. An approach which overcomes the conscious mind to the subconscious mind of the person. This is achieved by stressing the required phrase in a monotonous patterned approach.

5. Anchoring and sublimely programming the mind

This is the process of establishing an anchor in you so that it becomes easy to subject someone into a given state by sublimely programming the mind.

6. The proper way of applying hot words

The NLP professionals apply a certain sequence of words that appear normal but are more agreeable and suggestive. These words are linked with the senses. The words like hear this, eventually, see that, could immediately trigger a certain state of mind like feeling, imagining, and experiencing the desired perception in mind. They also apply certain vague terms to regulate thoughts.

7. Simple interpersonal subconscious mind programming

This implies that you dictate a person to plant a different thing in the subconscious mind of the subject.

This covert hypnosis approaches can affect the mind of people to a bigger extent but not to oblige them to do things that they are opposed to, which may demand a lot of mind programming.

4 NLP Tips to reconnect your brain

Change is difficult. So many of us struggle to shift from intention to action.

For instance, assume you want to quit smoking. You speak to yourself: It's such a bad thing, I need to stop. But wait, you have your birthday in a few weeks. You should wait. You know it will be tempting. I don't have any time to make any developments between now and then.

Can you see what happened there? In a few seconds, your thoughts go out of control. As you begin to think about a goal you wanted to accomplish, you went far ahead. Since you felt depressed, you procrastinated. You chose not to take action.

From a scientific point of view, procrastination is the means through which the brain controls stress. It is meant to protect us; our brains prevent us from achieving specific things that might be dangerous — things we consider as a big threat.

To make changes, we need to change how we think. With neurolinguistics programming, we can reconnect our thoughts and behavior.

One of the major tasks of an NLP practitioner is to highlight a person's favorite representational system. A person may prefer one sensory system to another. This can be established through language. For instance, if you like to say statements such as "I hear what you are saying," then that might show that you have a more auditory PRS instead of a visual PRS.

The five representational systems comprise:

1. Auditory
2. Visual
3. Kinesthetic
4. Olfactory
5. Gustatory

The language we apply reflect our subconscious perception of ourselves and the environment around us. In case our perception is incorrect, this generates a false internal belief system. Since our thoughts directly impact the way we think and behave, positive, permanent change begins with rewiring your brain.

The main aspect about beliefs is that it resembles a program that continues to run, where you continue to verify things whether it matches your beliefs or not.

So when your belief says that things are possible, and things will make you feel well, then what is going to take place is going to change your physiological differently than if you believe it is impossible. When you believe that things are difficult, you don't try, and you probably don't try with every fiber in your soul and every cell in your body.

Your beliefs are more powerful than what you always know. When your beliefs are strong, you can change your biochemistry. If you believe that medical treatment is going to heal you and it works, then you open yourself to every possibility.

If you want to close the gap between where you are and where you want to be, then here are some NLP tips that you can try today.

1. Do some affirmations

Why affirmations are great is because they work at every goal-setting stage.

You need to learn to say affirmations in the present tense because your subconscious mind will change the positive intention into reality, thus rewiring your brain faster.

Affirmations raise your self-awareness. By applying repetition, the new thoughts replace the old ones, making it ingrained in your mind. With sufficient practice, you can change your belief structure. This method is useful in addiction. When it comes to change, your brain requires to get on board first, and then over time, your body will follow.

2. Visualization

Are you aware that your brain cannot tell the difference between something imagined and something real? This means, your imagination is clear enough, you can convince your mind into experiencing positive emotions that match with a positive memory or mental picture. Determine the type of images that match with your goals.

Visualizations generate clarity to your dreams. The more positive visualizations you have, the more positive thoughts you experience, which will lead to positive behavior.

3. Content reframing

Try to recall a time when you felt angry or sad. For example, assume you ended a relationship. When you consider this, you are likely to experience negative emotions. To change your negative emotions to positive, you need to change the situation.

For instance, you are now open to a better relationship. The choice is yours to explore new options, and you have emerged from this challenge as a stronger and better person.

It is normal to panic when you lose a job, but this only builds emotional turmoil. By changing your concentration and changing your perspective, you will feel at peace.

In a certain study, researchers analyzed a group of nursing and midwifery students who were divided into two groups. The NLP training was administered in five 2-hour sessions, and the groups were studied.

Both nursing and midwifery group revealed differences in the scores of mental health, social function, and depression. It was concluded that NLP strategies are important in the enhancement of general health and different dimensions.

4. Anchoring

In this technique, you link a positive emotion to a certain phrase. This makes your brain to relate positive feeling with the gesture.

First, consider the emotion you want to feel. Decide whether you want to become confident, calmer, or happier?

Next, remember the last time you experienced that emotion.

Then, select an anchoring phrase like "I am happy. I am confident. I am calm."

Repeat this phrase daily until you can say the anchoring phrase and your mood changes to happy, confident, or calm.

Repetition is the key. The more you practice this method, the more it sticks in your mind. When you feel, think, visualize, and act by your intention, you will break the chain of negative habits.

The most important of all is to remember that these approaches are just tools. You have to work hard to experience positive effects continuously. For you to change, you have to decide to change.

Techniques of mind control

The notion that a mind can control objects excited people for several years. Psychic power study emerged during the cold war. During that time, there were rumors that the Russian were developing armies who had the psychic ability.

This rumor made the U.S government take action. The program known as Stargate was developed. Different tests were administered to determine whether or not the mind power can be important in military operations.

But none of these efforts proved the existence of psychokinesis. However, this does not mean that it is difficult to manipulate the mind.

Mind manipulation doesn't involve guiding objects or people to carry out illegal actions.

Before you can start to use the techniques of mind control, you need to understand your emotions first. Understand and master your emotions requires self-awareness. Learning to take charge of your emotions is the secret to manipulating others.

How can you manipulate people with your mind?

Mind manipulation requires that you ascertain why people behave in a certain way. This will provide you're the chance to examine one's emotion. Keep in mind that emotion is a powerful tool that determines human actions. Emotions make some people decide to commit suicide.

If you can make certain changes on an individual emotion, he or she will make the right steps based on his or her feelings. Marketers are the best when it comes to this. Since people like lower prices, businessmen don't reveal the actual price by quoting prices with two decimal places.

A five-dollar cup of coffee may look cheap if it is set at 4.99. Remember that there is no big difference between 5 and 4.99. However, many people prefer 4.99 over 5.

This marketing approach tends to work well all the time. It is the reason why you see this in the market.

Again, there are mind tricks applied here. It requires you to understand human emotion. If you understand how people act, it will be easier for you to take some action on their behavior.

How can you influence people?

Mind control isn't about making people understand or act in the manner you want them to go through your brain. Instead, it is about mastering their personality so that you can predict the individual's behavior in a given circumstance.

For example, if a co-worker shouts at you, look at him in the face silently. Stand straight like you are waiting for him to knock you. You will realize that he will stop and blackout. Why? Because he recognizes two things. First, you are not afraid. Next, he doesn't know what you are thinking. Your silence reveals deepness, which has no notion whether or not you are organizing an attack.

The calm water is fearless than a noisy one. In case the water is silent, it is deep. When it is deep, you cannot tell what lies below the surface. You cannot see it.

This analogy is correct to humans.

Additional mind control techniques

Fear: It is easy to threaten angry persons by demonstrating to them that you aren't afraid. This is not done by shouting. Instead, remain calm and silent and look at them at their eyes. The next thing will be interesting. You can push that person out without letting them do anything in response.

Guilt: Even the most notorious boss has a heart. She has softness inside. So if your boss is angry with you, you can make him, or her feel guilty. There are different ways. One of which is revealing to your boss that you are emotionally affected, you cannot focus on your job anymore. Once you do that, he or she will do everything to satisfy you.

Ego involvement: This works in an abusive relationship. You can let your abusive husband know that your friends are expecting a breakup, but you want to maintain his image that is why you stick in the relationship.

Anger: Anger is a great tool in changing mind and action. For example, if you are a leader of a team, and you always fail, you can trigger your team's perseverance by applying anger. Show them of who they are and their reason for taking this course. Once you trigger the better person in them, they will finish the rest.

Human emotion is weaker. It is fluid and always changing based on situational needs. If you know its mechanisms, you will know how to influence people, to guide them in the right direction, or to your advantage.

But it does not imply that you need to take advantage of others weakness to achieve what you want from them. Your main focus is to put yourself in the right direction.

Controlling others mind is not the same as making them follow anything that you want them to do. Nor deny them of being free and capable of making personal decisions.

Learning how to manipulate others makes you apply extra care and become clever. People who are good at influencing others know of themselves. And because they know themselves, they still know the behavior of others in any given situation.

Mirroring

Mirroring is a great technique that is used out there. It provides you with a hint of how our unconscious minds function below our level of awareness and the way we make decisions and judgments about someone without knowing the reason.

Mirroring, as the name goes, means emulating the other person and emulating the other person's gestures, the voice tone, or even phrases that may constitute mirroring. There are a lot of benefits of mirroring as long as you carry it in the right way.

The basic concept of mirroring

Do you know why we hate spiders, centipedes but feel okay around other mammals?

One reason is that other mammals resemble us than insects.

We are hard-wired to feel comfortable around other humans. This has an evolutionary benefit because the closer we live with other human beings, the higher the chances of survival.

Hence the more an organism is different from humans, the more comfortable we feel. In other words, our unconscious mind has learned to make us comfortable around those who look like us or share some similarity with us.

This is the reason why you enjoy when you meet a person whom you share ethnic background or cultural background in a foreign country. Or why you decide to sit with the people you know when you step into a room full of strangers.

This fact is what is learned in the NLP mirroring technique.

How mirroring is implemented

When it comes to mirrors, we try to persuade the subconscious mind of the other individual that we are similar to them. If it works, the person feels relaxed around us and may even begin to like us without knowing the reason.

The next time you converse with someone, try to pay attention to the body language of both of you. You will realize that you have taken the same gestures that are mirror images of the other. Your hands could be at the same position, or your legs may be crossed in the same manner.

All this takes place unconsciously as we feel relaxed around someone. However, this behavior can also happen in reverse, as in mirrors.

When it comes to mirrors, we emulate the gestures of the other person consciously to make them feel comfortable around us, even if they didn't feel that way at the start.

While you attempt to mirror someone during a conversation, you cannot suddenly copy their gestures because they may become suspicious. You are talking with their unconscious mind, so you need to do it slowly, so that is unnoticeable to their conscious mind.

If you want to ensure that your mirroring is successful, and the other person feels comfortable, you can always test it by making a new gesture. If the person unconsciously mirrors you, then your mirroring trial has been successful.

In addition to mirroring gestures, you can still influence the unconscious mind of the person of your similarity by applying the same tone of voice or speaking about common interests.

Still, repeating the words that the other person says can result in successful mirroring. For example, if they say "yes," you say "yes," when they say "no," you say "no."

The main thing is to do it moderately and regularly, without making the other person feel suspicious.

Can you remember how you smiled when the other person showed you that "TalkingTom" app in which the cat repeats the exact words you say to it?

This app became very popular, and there are many versions available now. All this uses the principle of mirroring.

Assume all the benefits you can get by making a person feel relaxed around you. If you are a salesperson, then the probabilities of making a sale can dramatically change if the customer feels comfortable around you.

In a business environment, the success of your negotiation depends to a huge extent on the level of comfort you can make the other person feel.

In conclusion, you should be careful while using mirroring. In other words, use it only when needed. While mirroring in itself is a manipulation technique, it is better that you use it in a win-win situation where you understand what you are doing is right for both of you or at least the person is not hurt in any way.

Here are a few ways someone is using mind control on you

1. Isolation

If you find yourself being isolated from your friends and family, then this is a cool sign that someone is attempting to control your mind. Your nearest and dearest will no doubt reveal to you what is wrong with your new friend and that is exactly what they don't want. They want you to stay alone and become vulnerable to break your spirit.

2. Moody behavior

Does your partner sulk if he or she fails to get what they wanted? Do you like to change your behavior to prevent an argument? This is the start of mind control, where your actions change because of what the other person does. It is a great sign that they are attempting to control your mind and are quite successful in it.

3. Metacommunication

This method is where a person sends subtle clues and hints using nonverbal cues. For example, if a husband asks his wide if she is fine and she responds 'yes' with a sigh and a shrug of her shoulders, this clearly shows that she is not fine, but her verbal response is positive. Some people apply metacommunication to generate subliminal thoughts.

4. Uncompromising rules

Does your partner apply unreasonable rules on your lifestyle? If you are required to complete impossible deadlines, have strict mealtimes and bathroom breaks, then this is mind control.

What they are doing is denying you all your decisions so that you follow a strict set of behaviors. This will stop you thinking for yourself and make it easier for them to implant their ideas.

Can you stop mind control?

The response is yes, and we need to be alert to use these strategies in different situations to manage to prevent mind control from taking place.

Keep a close eye for discontinuities between somebody's ideas and their actual behaviors. In case what they say does not match what they do, be vigilant.

Study communications, look for any hidden agendas behind the general content.

Be ready to disobey simple situational rules or polite social customs if you think it is important.

Look out for situational and group pressures in your social and physical environment.

Don't do anything unusual or anything that you don't want to do to satisfy others.

Understand the conditions in which you are vulnerable — major life activities, depression, grief, loss, losing a job, and so forth.

Don't be forced to make a decision. Reserve the right to defer a decision or say no.

If you think you need extra information, do so. Or search for other informational sources.

Effective persuaders look like us. Be very careful of excessive emphasis on topics of mutual interests to stop mind control before it is too late.

Be worried about requests to take part in small commitment.

Pay attention while in social gatherings to find out who is controlling who, and why.

In case there is a disagreement, say your arguments with conviction. If necessary, practice creative arguments, and listen to persuasive messages to avoid accepting them.

Emotional manipulation

When our attention is directed towards us by being made to feel wrong or bad, we tend to become self-conscious, and we start to think what others may think of us. This makes us more vulnerable to mind control.

Professional manipulators influence our emotions. Be careful of people who start emotion-laden conflicts, particularly if they are delivering a solution.

Don't confess to anything or reveal information that can later be used against you.

Avoid making decisions while feeling depressed, especially when you are in the presence of the individual, causing stress.

When you experience extreme emotions, your ability to think critically reduces. Do whatever you need to do to relax, even if it demands to leave the situation.

Pay attention to those who create fear and guilt. These are strong emotions for changing your beliefs and attitudes.

If a person says that he or she is making sacrifices on your behalf, thank them with words.

Groups

Be wary if you tend to make a lot of good friends very fast in a new group. If someone makes you feel intelligent, special and constantly tells you that you will do well with them, you need to re-evaluate what is going on if you need to stop mind control early in the process.

If you are being replied with simple, complete answers to difficult problems, it should be interpreted as a warning sign. "Simply do this, and your life will be different!"

If someone tells you that you need to step out of your mind, or your problems revolve around your thinking, be careful that it is not a means of generating a state of passive acceptance.

Decisions

You should listen to warning bells and see flashing lights when a person stresses your freedom of choice of the alternatives provided.

Also, when they say that you have lost some freedom, but with them, you can get it back again, particularly when you feel powerful that you need it.

Review any commitments and decisions you made in the past if they are no longer important.

A strong self-worth

Learn to maintain your self-worth, even in frustrating situations.

Do not accept the idea that someone is more competent than you.

Don't accept generalizations to your questions. Complex communication doesn't make conclusions acceptable. Be careful too, semantic distortion and jargon.

Always look out for criticisms before you join a group and invest your time and money.

Learn to identify the tricks in the language used, for instance, advertisements.

Avoid negative dialogue about yourself, particularly if it developed by somebody else.

Be careful of people who mirror your body language

If you are talking to a person who could be into NLP, and you realize that they are sitting in the same way as you, or copying the way you have your hands, test them by changing your position and see whether they do the same thing. Experts in NLP will be effective at this than newer ones, but new ones will instantly mirror your new movement. This is a great time to call people on their shit.

Do not allow anyone to touch you

This looks obvious and natural. However, let us pretend that you are talking to somebody you know is learning NLP, and you find yourself in a strong emotional state-maybe you start to get angry or laugh hard and the person you are talking to touches you while you are in that state. For instance, they may touch you on the shoulder. What just took place? They anchored you so that later on when they want to put you back into the previous state, they can touch you in the same place.

Be careful of permissive language

"Be free to relax." You are welcome to take a look at this phone. You can enjoy this as much as you want." Watch out for this. This is a powerful insight into pre-NLP. The best way to make someone do something, including going into a trance, is permitting them to do so. However, experienced hypnotists will not command you to do something. Instead, they will say things like, "Feel free to become as comfortable as you want."

Read between the lines

NLP persons will regularly employ a language with hidden or layered meanings. For example, "Diet, nutrition, and sleep with me are the most crucial things, don't you think so?" On the surface, if you heard this, it would appear like a normal sentence that you would perhaps agree without extra thought. Of course, diet, sleep, and nutrition are key things, and this person is into being healthy, that is great. However, what is highlighted in the message?" Nutrition, diet, and sleep with me are the most critical things, and you unconsciously agreed to it. Expert NLPers can be subtle with this.

Be careful of vague language

One of the main techniques that NLP borrowed from Milton Erickson is the application of vague language to generate hypnotic trance. Erickson discovered that the vaguer language is, the more it makes people get into a trance because there is less than an individual is liable to disagree with or respond to. Similarly, the more specific language will take a person out of the trance.

Be careful of gibberish

Phrases such as "As you continue to release this feeling, the more you will find yourself shifting into present alignment with the sound of your success more and more." This type of gibberish is the leading phase of NLP. There is nothing that the hypnotist is saying; they are simply trying to control your internal emotional state and take you where they want you to go. Learn to say, "Can you be more elaborate about that" or "Can you explain exactly what you mean?"

This achieves two things: it interrupts this entire technique, and it also forces the conversation into a specific language, ending the trance-inducing application of vague language.

Don't say yes to everything

If you find yourself being directed to make a hasty decision on something, and feel like you are being steered, avoid the situation. Wait for 24 hours before you make any decision, particularly financial ones. Do not allow yourself to be swayed into making an emotional decision instantly. Salespeople have NLP techniques, particularly for engineering impulse buys. Don't do it. Leave and apply your rational mind.

Always trust your intuition

The primary rule is always to trust what your gut tells you. So if your intuition tells you that someone is fucking with you, trust it.

Hopefully, these tips will help you to resist this annoying and modern art of black magic.

Chapter 6: Mind Manipulation-Persuasion

Understanding Persuasion

Persuasion is probably one of the most misunderstood terms in the present culture. People look at persuaders as phony guys dressed in suits, attempting to convince people to buy or do something that only benefits the persuaders alone.

But the truth is that good persuasion involves helping others. There are many reasons why being persuasive is necessary for business life and personal life. Most importantly, persuasion allows people to take actions that will benefit them despite the mental obstacles they may face that prevent them from doing so.

The baseline is that individuals won't purchase your product or service unless they are persuaded to do so. The same is true with vendors, investors and business partners. That is the reason why persuasion is an indispensable business skill in the current world.

Here's how being persuasive, and why every professional should learn how to persuade.

First, **what does it mean to be persuasive**

Regardless of what circumstances we go through in life; persuasion always plays a big role in the result. You could be attempting to persuade a toddler to brush their teeth, persuading a friend to come for dinner at a given restaurant you love, or getting your friend to come to your home at a certain time of the day. It doesn't matter who we are, or what we do; we all try to persuade someone at some point.

When it comes to business, persuasion happens every day. Advertising is a form of persuasion by trying to convince customers to come to your store or use your services. Persuasion is also important to any negotiation, and for businesses, this can imply persuading vendors to deliver better services. And consider working with staff, you are always persuading them to increase their effort, and take on new tasks.

Why does persuasion have a negative connotation

Sometimes, persuasion is viewed by people as a "dirty word" in society. To some people, "persuasion" means manipulating, and pressuring someone. Normally, the age-old "used car salesman" stereotype is often triggered when people consider persuasion. But this could be far from the truth.

Consider persuasion as an extension of effective communication. By expertly describing the importance and logic of something to gain an agreement or create a consensus, excellent persuaders can develop a win-win for everyone. You could be persuading others how a given proposal makes sense, and the various ways it benefits other parties. Part of business persuasion is revealing to stakeholders how a business will produce returns or telling employees why a new approach will benefit them in the long run.

It is all about learning how different process analyses information and communicate in a manner that is best for them. However, negative stigma is the persuasion considered as manipulative or dishonest. People are worried of persuasive individuals attempting to sell them something they don't need, or worse yet is a defective product.

Why persuasion is a good thing, and how to become better at it

It is critical to have a clear knowledge of persuasion. Persuasion isn't just convincing people to do something they aren't willing to do or isn't in their interest.

Persuasion means crafting a clear, logical case for why an individual should do something, describing the facts and allowing people to make their conclusions.

Below are important tips you can use to become more persuasive, in either personal or professional environment:

- **Be a great listener:** it is a misconception that persuasion involves you talking. Being a great listener implies giving people your complete attention. Look them in the eye and repeat their name throughout the conversation. Let them finish before you interject. This shows that you are more trustworthy and more of a consultant individual.

- **Do enough research:** For you to persuade someone properly, you need to build credibility. By conducting your homework, creating pertinent facts, and coming out as an expert in the field, people will become receptive to your message.

- **Address fears:** Every persuader encounters objections, and solving them is perhaps the most important feature of persuasion. If a person disagrees with you, don't just move forward with your pitch. Try to understand why they feel that way, allow them to understand your view, and describe rationally how your solution will ultimately erase their fears.

- **Display empathy:** Empathy is the secret to persuasion because you are trying to solve someone's issues, or exclude one of their pain points. Put yourself in their shoes, know where they want to go, and how badly they want to reach there. Let them know that you understand how they feel, and if you have a bad experience, proceed to share it with them. Empathy builds trust and connection that is important to great persuasion.

So far, you need to have a good foundation of why you need to be persuasive. Keep in mind that top persuaders develop a bulletproof logical case. However, they know how critical emotion plays in presentation and delivery. Persuasion isn't just selling someone a used a car. It is about being a great listener, knowing the exact problems people go through, and creating a solution that benefits everyone.

Why persuasion is critical in the negotiation

Negotiating involves reaching an agreement based on a particular issue and one of the important skills, in this case, is the ability to convince another.

Persuasion skills are important in a successful negotiation. You must learn to persuade your counterpart to accept your position. Through mastering important negotiation skills, you can learn the skill of persuasion to influence your counterpart.

For you to negotiate successfully, you need to learn the art of persuasion. You need to learn how to persuade others to accept your opinions. Additionally, you need to know how to persuade others to change their opinions effectively. Persuasion and other features of negotiation are considered as talents by some, but they are skills that can be practiced between friends, or colleagues, or even learned online using tutorials.

Mastering the skill of persuasion requires you to deal with disputes during a negotiation. The skill is not limited to business negotiations. It can assist in resolving political challenges.

Now that you know why persuasion is critical in a negotiation, let us look at how you can concentrate on using these persuasion skills to affect the result of a negotiation positively.

1. Build self-confidence

To convince others to accept your opinion, you must trust yourself. You have to learn to be confident. Once you master this skill, you will be able to convince the counterpart. You will understand how to carefully look at things and decide which decision best fits you.

2. Highlight the benefits

For you to successfully persuade others, you need to point out the benefits of the proposal to the other individual. You must respond to this question, "What's in it for me?" Replying to this question will assist you in fitting the proposal with the interests of the other party.

3. Learn to counter critics actively

The biggest mistake in a negotiation is to assume that everything will run well without any objection from the other party. However, this is not always the case. You need to expect to get criticisms from your counterpart. This is part of the negotiation.

If you expect criticisms from the other side, then it is hard to be found unaware. Being ready will offer you a chance to understand and address any questions from the other party quickly. This way, you will convert objections into strengths that will create a means to a successful negotiation.

Principles of persuasion

Researchers have been looking at factors that make us say "yes" to other requests for over 60 years. There is no question that there's science to how we are convinced, and that science will shock you.

When you make a decision, it would be great to think that people factor all the available information to guide their thinking. But the truth is always different. In the overloaded lives we live, we need shortcuts to direct our decision-making.

Mastering these shortcuts and ethically using them can be important in raising the chances that someone will be convinced by your request.

Let us dive deeper and look at each principle of persuasion.

1. Reciprocity

People always feel obliged to extend back favor done to them by their friends. This can be a gift they were given or a service they received.

In case a friend invites you to attend their party, the next time you host a party you will want to invite them to also come to your party. If a colleague sends you a gift, then you owe that colleague a gift. And in a social setting, people are likely to acknowledge those they owe.

The best proof of this principle is from studies done in restaurants. There is a high chance the last time you visited a restaurant the waiter offered you a gift while handing you the bill.

The question is, does this small gift have any effect on the amount of tip you are going to leave them? Many people will say no. However, that gift can have a huge difference. In the research, providing customers in a restaurant, a single mint at the end of their meal increased tips by 3%.

The main secret to using this principle is that you must be the first to give and ensure that it is unexpected and personalized.

2. Scarcity

Did you know that people want more of the scarce things?

The time British Airways released an announcement in 2003 that they are going to remove the twice-daily London-New York Concorde flight because of economic reasons. Sales skyrocketed the next day.

Pay attention that nothing had changed concerning the Concorde itself. The service didn't get super, and the flight didn't get faster. It had only become a rare resource. And so, people wanted to take advantage of it.

This means, when you want to effectively convince people using this principle, you need to make something scarce. Don't just tell people all the benefits they will earn if they choose your services and products. You will need to highlight the special benefits and what they may miss if they don't buy your product.

3. Authority

When people see you as an expert in a field, others will be more likely to oppose you. Why? Usually, experts can present a shortcut to better decisions that would instead take long to develop. The concept then is to develop that authority and expertise.

Most people miss this chance because they assume others will recognize their expertise. You can't leave it up for others to interpret for themselves because it will be overlooked.

There are different ways to create authority. A quick and easy one is to display your awards and credentials in the office or your workplace. Perhaps, this may not always be the way out. Another approach is to deliver expertise using short anecdotes in casual conversations.

Keep in mind your expertise isn't always a known thing, so you need to relay it when you get an opportunity.

4. Liking

People like those who consider them as friends. It is a simple but powerful principle. This principle can be used in several ways.

One way is to identify a common factor with the people you encounter. If you can interact with them on their interests, you will have a solid foundation to build from. Being keen on people is an excellent way to identify clues that may create this common factor.

The other way is to use honest praise. Complimenting people and being charming build a positive connection with others. But you need to be careful so that you don't exaggerate. The point here is genuine praise.

5. Consistency

This principle is defined by the power of active and voluntary commitments, which makes people stick to their word. Let us explore these requirements. First, there is an active commitment. This means something that is spoken to others. Having people pledge that they will do a certain thing is a great start, but when they actively stick to it, they are likely to follow through.

The next part is to make it public. When others look at the following commitment, it increases the level of accountability to the statement. And nobody wants to return to their word.

6. Social proof

People depend on social hints from others on how to feel, think and respond in many instances. And not just any person, but peers. People know they are similar. This is referred to as social proof.

Therefore, if your goal is to influence a certain team in your department, you have to get one of them to purchase first. Once they see this kind of employee taking action on their own, they are likely to do the same.

Letting the first person take action creates the difference and opens the power of social proof.

Finally, if you can integrate all these to create a situation, your power of persuasion will increase by a big percent.

Learning and mastering the six principles of influence will allow you to optimize your strengths of persuasion. But a word of caution. Use these principles well; don't abuse them. They can easily be used to manipulate and influence others emotionally.

Chapter 7: Hypnosis techniques

Just like brainwashing is a form of mind control, hypnosis is an important type that cannot be ignored. For the most part, those who have some knowledge about hypnosis learned it from watching stage shows of members performing ridiculous acts. Although this is a form of hypnosis, there is more to it. This chapter will focus on hypnosis as a method of mind control.

Well, **what is hypnosis?**

Let us start by defining hypnosis. Experts consider hypnosis as a state of consciousness that requires focused attention along with the reduced level of awareness that is demonstrated by the participant increased capacity to respond to suggestions created. This implies that the participant is going to get into a separate state of mind and will be much more vulnerable to following the suggestions given by the hypnotist.

It is widely understood that two theory groups explain what happens during a hypnosis process. The first is referred to as the altered state theory.

Those who apply this theory look at hypnosis as a state of mind that is altered where the participant will see that their awareness is different from what they would see in their normal conscious state.

The other theory is the non-state theories. Those who implement this theory don't believe that those who undergo hypnosis enter into a different state of consciousness.

However, the participant works with the hypnotist to get into a state of imaginative role enactment.

Although in hypnosis, the participant is considered to have more attention and combines with the new ability to concentrate on a particular memory, or thought intensely. During this process, the participant can block out other sources that might distract them.

The hypnotized members are said to reveal a heightened ability to reply to suggestions that are directed to them, particularly when these suggestions originate from the hypnotist. The process that is applied to place the participant into hypnosis is referred to as hypnotic induction and will require a sequence of suggestions and instructions that are used as a warm-up.

Numerous thoughts are created by the experts as to what the definition of hypnosis is. The different types of these definitions arise from the fact that various situations come with hypnosis, and no one person has the same experience when they are going through it. Some of the different definitions of hypnosis by professionals include:

1. A special instance of psychological regression.
2. A means of the body to dissociate from itself in a separate plane of consciousness.

Some many different statements and views have been said about hypnosis. Some people think hypnosis is real and are afraid that the government and others around them will try to influence their minds.

Others don't believe in hypnosis at all and consider it just sleight of hand. In most cases, the concept of hypnosis as a mind control falls somewhere in the middle.

There are three steps of hypnosis that are considered by the psychological community.

These three stages consist of hypnosis that is considered by the psychological community. These three stages comprise of suggestion, induction, and susceptibility. Each of them is critical to the hypnosis process and will be explored further.

Induction

The first step of hypnosis is induction. Before the participant goes through the complete hypnosis, they will be introduced to the hypnotic induction technique. For many years, this was believed as the method used to subject the targets into their hypnotic trance, but that definition has changed. Some non-state theorists have experienced this stage slightly differently. Instead, they consider this step as a means to increase the participants' expectations of what is happening, defining the role that they will play, getting their attention to concentrate in the right direction and any of the other steps required to guide the participant into the correct direction for hypnosis.

Different induction approaches can be applied during hypnosis. The most popular and influential method is Braid's "eye-fixation" approach or "Braidism." There are different variations of this method, including the Stanford Hypnotic Susceptibility Scale (this). This scale is a commonly used tool for research in the field of hypnosis.

To apply the Braid induction techniques, you will need to follow several steps. The first one is to take any object that you can find that is bright, like a watch case, and hold it between the middle, fore, and thumb fingers on the left hand.

You will need to hold this object about 8-15 inches from the eyes of the participant. Hold the object above the forehead so that it generates a lot of strain on the eyelids and eyes during the process so that the participant can maintain a fixed stare on the object at all times.

The hypnotist must then tell the participant always to keep their eyes fixed on to the object. The patient will also need to concentrate their mind completely on the idea of a given object. They should not be permitted to think of other things, or allow their minds and eyes to wander, or else the process will not be successful.

After some time, the participant's eyes will start to dilate. Then the participant will start to assume a wavy motion.

In case the participant involuntarily closes their eyelids when the middle and forefingers of the right hand are transferred from the eyes to the object, then they are in a trance. If not, then the participant will have to start again. Make sure you allow the participant to know that they can close their eyes once the fingers are transferred in the same motion back to the eyes. This will make the patient assume the altered state of mind that is referred to as hypnosis.

Although Braid supported his technique, he did accept that using the induction technique of hypnosis is not always important for every situation. Researchers in the modern era have often found that the induction technique isn't as important to the effects of hypnotic suggestion as previously thought.

With time, other means of the original hypnotic induction technique have been created, although the Brain method is still considered as the best.

Suggestion

The next step of hypnosis is called suggestion. The first time hypnosis was described by James Braid; the word suggestion was not used.

However, Braid referred to this stage as the process of having the conscious mind of the participant concentrate on one dominant idea. How Braid accomplished, this was to activate or limit the physiological functioning of the different parts of the participant's body. Later on, Braid started to emphasize the application of different non-verbal and verbal forms of suggestion to get the participant into the state of mind.

These would involve employing "waking suggestions" plus self-hypnosis.

Another famous hypnotist, Hippolyte Bernheim, continued to change the emphasis of the physical state of the process of hypnosis over to the psychological process that featured verbal suggestions. Bernheim believes that hypnotism is the induction of a physical condition that is unique and which will boost the susceptibility of the suggestion to the participant.

He stated, the hypnotic state that is stimulated will help to facilitate the suggestion, although this may not be necessary to begin the susceptibility in the first place.

The modern hypnotism applies many different suggestion forms to become successful such as insinuations, metaphors, and non-verbal suggestions, and other figures of speech and suggestions that are non-verbal.

Some of the non-verbal suggestions that could be applied during the suggestion stage would involve physical manipulation, mental imagery, and voice tonality.

One of the distinctions that are created in the types of suggestion that can be presented to the participant include suggestions that are delivered with permission and those that are more authoritarian.

One of the things that have been taken into consideration about hypnosis is the difference between the unconscious and the conscious mind.

Different hypnotists consider the stage of suggestion as a means of communicating that is guided for the most part to the conscious state of the subject.

Others in the field will see it differently; they see the communication taking place between the agent and the subconscious or unconscious mind.

Proponents of the first class of thought include Braid, Bernheim, and other pioneers of the Victorian age. They believed that the suggestions were being directed to the conscious part of the subjects' mind instead of the unconscious part. Braids go on to define the act of hypnotism as the total attention to the suggestion or dominant concept. The worry of most people that hypnotists will get into their unconscious and make them perform and think things beyond their control is impossible according to those who adhere to this train of thought.

The state of mind has also been determinant of the various conceptions about the suggestion. Those who believed that the responses given are through the unconscious mind, like the case of Milton Erickson. Many of these indirect suggestions, such as metaphors, will encrypt their intended meaning to hide it from the conscious mind of the subject. The subliminal suggestion is a method of hypnosis that depends wholly on the theory of the unconscious mind. If the unconscious mind were not part of the hypnosis, this suggestion would not be possible. The difference between the two groups is fairly easy to identify. Those that believe that the suggestions will shift to the conscious mind will employ direct verbal instructions, and those that believe the suggestions will head to the unconscious mind will use metaphors and stories with hidden meanings.

In both of these theories of thought, the participant will need to concentrate on a single object or idea. This allows them to be guided in the direction that is needed to enter the hypnotic state. Once the suggestion stage is done successfully, the participant can then move into the third stage of susceptibility.

Susceptibility

With time, it has been found that people will respond differently to hypnosis. Some people realize that they can fall into a hypnotic trance quite easily and do not need to put a lot of effort into the process at all. Others find that they can get into the hypnotic trance, but only after some time and with some effort. Still, some find that they cannot get into the hypnotic trance, and even after putting more effort they cannot attain their goals. One thing that has intrigued researchers about the susceptibility of different subjects is that this aspect remains constant. If you have managed to get into a hypnotic state of mind, you are likely to remain the same way for the rest of your life. On the flip side, if you have always had problems reaching the hypnotic state and have never been hypnotized, then there is a great chance that you will never.

There have been different models created to try and determine the susceptibility of participants to hypnosis. Some of the older depth scales worked on inferring the state of trance the members were in through observable signs that were present. These would include things like spontaneous amnesia. Some of the modern scales of work to determine the level of self-evaluated or observed responsiveness to the particular suggestion tests that are provided, such as the direct suggestions of arm rigidity.

Based on research done by Deirdre Barrett, there are two subjects considered as highly susceptible to the effects of hypnotism. These two groups comprise of dissociation and fantasizers. The fantasizers will record high scores on the absorption scales, will be able to block out the stimuli of the real world without the application of hypnosis.

On the other hand, there are dissociates. This group will always come from a background of trauma or childhood abuse, learn ways to forget the unpleasant events that are in their past, and can disappear into numbness. If an individual in this group daydream, it is more in terms of going blank rather than building fantasies. Both of these groups score high on tests of hypnotic susceptibility. The two groups that have the highest rates of hypnotizability include those experiencing posttraumatic stress disorder and dissociative identity disorder.

Applications

Hypnosis is an idea that has been in existence for a long time. As a result, different applications have started to pop up that make use of hypnosis. The different applications of hypnosis cross many areas such as entertainment, military uses self-improvement, and medical benefits.

Other fields that have recently started to incorporate hypnosis include physical therapy, hypnotism, sports, education, and forensics. Even artists have started to apply hypnotism to accomplish specific creative purposes. This is demonstrated mostly by Andre Breton, who has used hypnosis among other approaches for his creative functions.

One of the increasing uses of hypnosis is in the field of self-improvement. Many people have decided to perform self-hypnosis to help them reduce stress, lose weight, and quit smoking.

Let us look at the different fields where hypnosis is used and how it is being applied.

Hypnotherapy

Here is where hypnosis is applied as a means of psychotherapy. It is used as a means to help the patient or subject through tough issues that are disturbing them, particularly when other methods of self-control aren't effective.

Authorized psychologists and physicians may perform a form of hypnotherapy on patients to treat posttraumatic stress, sleep disorders, anxiety, compulsive gambling, and depression.

It is also possible to get in touch with a hypnotherapist to help you address problems such as weight management and the cessation of smoking. If you visit a certified hypnotherapist, it is important to recall that they are not psychologists so they will be able to help you with attaining the hypnotic state and not with curing your more serious ailments. It is better that you ensure whoever you are working with has been accredited to provide you with these services, whether you select a hypnotherapist or a physician.

The process of hypnotherapy has been seen in different methods in modern history.

All of them have had different degrees of success, depending on the problem faced and the participants. Some of the ways that have been used consist of:

- Cognitive-behavioral therapy. This is a mix of clinical hypnosis plus different elements of Cognitive Behavioral Therapy.

- Hypnoanalysis. Also known as the age of regression.

- Hypnosis to help address fears and phobias.

- Hypnotherapy to treat addictions.

- Hypnotherapy to deal with pain management in those who experience chronic pain.

- Hypnotherapy to help with relaxation

- Hypnotherapy to treat psychological therapy the patient is battling with.

- Hypnotherapy to help with habit control

- Hypnotherapy to help with weight loss

- Hypnotherapy to sooth patients anxious about going through surgery.

Military applications

Besides helping people deal with different health problems and addiction, people have been wondering whether hypnosis has been employed by military and government officials to change how citizens think about things.

So far, there has been minimal proof that the American military has used hypnosis to accomplish their goals. A declassified source that was extracted from the Freedom of Information Act archive reveals that the process of hypnosis has been investigated for application in military applications.

Despite the research that has been conducted, the study concluded that there was no evidence to show that hypnosis would be helpful in military application. Additionally, there was evidence that demonstrated hypnosis existed.

The source further explains how it would be difficult to apply hypnosis in the military.

It states, "The use of hypnosis in intelligence would present certain technical problems

not encountered in the clinic or laboratory."

Self-hypnosis

There are some situations, such as when a certain professional is not present, when you may choose to use the process of self-hypnosis. This process happens when an individual can hypnotize themselves, usually using the technique of autosuggestion.

The main application for this technique is for self-improvement, and many people will practice it to reduce their stress levels, stop smoking, or attain the motivation they need to continue on a diet. Although some people can self-hypnotize, most people need some help to reach this state. This may include hypnotic recordings or even mind machine devices to assist them to hit that state. Other fields that you could apply self-hypnosis include your general physical well-being, to relax, and to overcome stage fright.

Stage hypnosis

When people look at hypnosis, they recall stage hypnosis. This is a means of entertainment that will take place in a theatre or a club in front of an audience. The hypnotist is always presented with a great showman, and this spreads the notion that hypnosis is fully about mind control. At the start, the hypnotist will try to subject the entire audience under the altered state before selecting specific people who satisfy the criteria to come on the stage and go through various embarrassing acts while the remaining group watches.

It is unclear why stage hypnosis is so effective while it is commonly considered as a combination of trickery, physical manipulation, psychological factors, and participant selection.

For the most parts, experts believe that the participant is only playing along with the hypnotist and providing a great show.

These people could be ready to do this because they wish to be in the middle of all the attention, the desire to please others, and the excuse to oppose their suppressors of fear making it easy to get the participants to act.

Popular books written by former stage hypnotists emphasize the notion of trickery and deception, and some are composed of fake hypnosis where private whispers are used the whole time.

Types of hypnosis

There are different types of hypnosis that a target will undergo. Each of them will work differently, and some of the work to attempt to solve various problems. Some may be fit to help the target relax while others can help more with weight loss or pain management. Let us dive deep into the different types of hypnosis.

Traditional hypnosis

This is the most common type of hypnosis. In this process, the agent sends suggestions directly to the target's unconscious mind. This form of hypnosis will work well on a subject who is known for acknowledging the things that they are told, and they don't question a lot. If you decide to visit an authorized hypnotist or buy a tape to complete the process of self-hypnosis, you will be going undergoing traditional hypnosis. The reason that this form of hypnosis is popular is that it does not take a lot of experience or training to learn how to do. The hypnotist is only going to write a simple script and inform the subject of what to do. Although this technique will work well on those who accept what is happening around them, it is ineffective for those who think analytically and critically.

Embedded technique

During this process, the hypnotist will narrate to the subject an interesting story. This story is supposed to help distract and involve the conscious mind of the subject. It will also have indirect suggestions that are hidden within the story but which will be acknowledged into the unconscious mind of the subject. Through this story, the hypnotist will rely on process instructions to guide the unconscious mind of the subject to identify the memory that is needed. This memory is always about learning new experiences that are right from the past.

The hypnotist will then apply that learning experience to help them make changes to their present.

Ericksonian hypnosis

This type of hypnosis is a bit deep because it is going to demand the application of metaphors and little stories. These are applied to present the ideas and suggestions that are needed by the unconscious mind. Although this method requires some experience and training to do, it is effective and excellent to use.

Why it works so well is because it can eliminate the resistance and blockage that the target may have to the suggestions.

Two kinds of metaphors will always be used in this type of hypnosis.

- Interspersal
- Isomorphic

For the interspersal metaphor, the instruction that is explained has been included in the story and would not be easily recognized by the subject outside of their unconscious mind. The other metaphor is more common and provides directions to the unconscious mind by presenting a story to the subject that will present a moral at the end.

The unconscious mind will draw a one to one relationship linking the elements that come from the story and the elements that come with the behavior or problem.

Example of isomorphic metaphor is "Boy Who Cried, Wolf." Many parents use this story to enlighten their children about lying, particularly if their child speaks a lot of lies. After listening to the story, the unconscious mind of the subject would identify a parallel between speaking lies and the boy in the story. They would see that telling lies may lead to a disaster, and the child may be ready to stop lying in the process to avoid that disaster from taking place.

Neuro-linguistic programming

With NLP, hypnotists have a huge selection of the methods that they use in the hypnosis process.

When applying the process of NLP, the hypnotist will employ the same thought patterns that are creating the issue in the subject. This can save a lot of time compared to undergoing the process of suggestion. For instance, the thought patterns that are used with an excessive appetite will be used to help solve the problem that the subject is handling. If it used with a qualified hypnotist, NLP is very effective.

Many forms of NLP programming have been used by hypnotists. Some of the most common forms of NLP include anchoring, NLP Reframe, and NLP Flash,

NLP Anchoring

A great way to consider to understand how these anchoring works are to consider an old song that you know.

Have you ever been relaxing in a car and heard a song that you have never heard for quite some time? Did that song awaken some feeling in your that came from the past?

The first time you heard that song, you experience these feelings and the unconscious mind connected these feelings to that particular song. In this process, the song would become the anchor for these feelings.

Now, every time that you hear this song, you will stimulate the brain to have these feelings all over again. This is a great example of anchoring.

Most hypnotists have discovered that anchoring is an important technique for them to apply in hypnotizing their subjects. For instance, if you have a memory of being gifted a present for doing something good in the past, the hypnotist will get into that memory to help you recreate the feel that you were experiencing at the time.

Alternatively, the hypnotist will have you perform some action like touching your two fingers together during the recreation of the process.

Now every time that you touch your fingers together, you will experience those same happy feelings.

The process of anchoring can work encourage you to complete something by connecting good feelings with it. For instance, this method is always used to help people get the motivation they deserve to continue to lose weight and stick to a diet.

The hypnotist will work with the subject to generate a positive anchor that is connected with the mental image of the subject. In the following case, it will be the subject thinking about themselves in a thin and sexy body. Once the subject imagines this image, they will awaken the anchor and acquire the positive motivation that they need. There is a sudden increase in the motivation for weight loss in those who go through hypnosis, unlike those who do not. The process of anchoring can be used in different ways to help in the self-improvement of the person.

NLP Flash

This is another type of hypnosis that is said to be very powerful and only performed by a qualified professional. It is always used to change the thoughts and feelings around the unconscious mind of the subject.

It can be an excellent way to help those who experience chronic stress or are addicted to a certain substance. In this case, the hypnotist will share the feelings of the subject around, instead of a given act generating pleasure, that act will begin to generate pain instead of another act generating stress, it will bring the subject relaxation. For instance, when a person is addicted to a substance like a cigarette or alcohol, it will experience a feeling of pleasure and happiness when they take that substance.

Using the technique of NLP flash, these feelings will be switched around, leading to the subject feeling uncomfortable or pain when they take the substance. This can help them to overcome their addiction effectively.

Those who go through a lot of stress have also identified the technique of NLP Flash to work well for them. When a person is experiencing chronic stress, they may have problems to control their blood pressure and their tempers. They will feel very uncomfortable all the time.

Since stress is so difficult on the body, there are many patients ready to undergo the NLP Flash hypnosis to help them relax. With the above technique, the subject will master their stress trigger and redirect them so that those triggers begin to produce feelings of relaxation in their minds.

This method has also shown to be effective in eliminating the conditioned responses in the mind of the subject. An example of this is with smoking. A smoker who enjoys a cigarette while having a cup of coffee in the morning, his or her unconscious brain is going to begin pairing these two behaviors together. This implies that the subject will crave to have a cigarette anytime they enjoy a cup of coffee, particularly in the morning.

When the subject experiences NLP Flash technique, they will learn how to differentiate the two events from each other.

This makes it possible for the smoker to get a cup of coffee without also getting the desire to smoke at the same time. This makes it more effective when attempting to quit smoking.

NLP Reframe

This is the third technique applied in hypnosis. This approach is potent because it works so well in helping the subject to change how they behave. To achieve this process, the hypnotist must know that there is a secondary gain or a positive outcome, that is achieved by each of the behaviors that a person does.

The result that happens from the behavior is important because that is the reason the subject acts. Regardless of the importance of the outcome, the behavior that is selected to achieve the result is not that important.

During the reframing process, the hypnotist works to negotiate and debate with the unconscious mind of the subject. The objective is to take over the responsibility for making the subject replace some new behavior that is available and effective at achieving the required secondary gain. While this happens in the subconscious, the new behavior will be acceptable to the subject in their conscious mind. For instance, if the person tends to eat when they are sad to make themselves feel better, the hypnotist is going to perform this method to teach the unconscious to carry out some activity. The act of eating can be substituted with exercise or reading an interesting book, assisting the subject in losing weight, eating a healthy diet, and feeling better all around.

Video Hypnosis

While the other methods of hypnosis are popular in helping the subjects overcome obstacles and change how they think to live better lives, new forms of hypnosis are always being created. One of the newest forms of hypnotherapy that has been created is video hypnosis. This method is delivered through financial means so that people can buy them and use them at their convenience. The methods used in certain brands of video hypnosis depend on Neuro-Linguistic Programming technology that we discussed earlier.

This implies that video hypnosis technique will work by taking advantage of the existing thought processes that the subject has instead of applying hypnotic suggestion like traditional methods.

Why this technique has become popular is because more than 70% of people have found that they learn things easier and quicker when they see things compared to only when they hear information. The minds of the subject will learn to change the feelings that it is experiencing as well as its visual connections automatically on the conscious level while watching at the visual movies presented.

Although there are several types of video hypnosis programs available, Neuro-vision is the most popular because it has been created using the best techniques in the industry.

This type of video method works to train the unconscious mind of the subject via digital optics, which is a high tech stimulation on the computer. This will free the subject of their urges, tensions, and compulsions. Through this process, the smoker will discover that stopping smoking is easy, the dieter will lose their appetite, and those who feel depressed will start to relax more. It will take at least a few sessions of video hypnosis to see the outcome, while some find that single view beginning to reveal the results that they want.

Subliminal hypnosis

The last type of hypnosis discussed in this chapter. Typically, subliminal hypnosis messages will be recorded for the subject to listen to. The recording will contain two types of tracks, and each one will talk to a different part of the mind.

One track will have a cover sound that will be heard through the conscious mind of the subject. The cover sound is always easy for the brain to listen to like nature, sounds or music. The other track will feature direct suggestions that will be heard through the unconscious mind of the subject. These suggestions are available on the second track that will be repeated over and over throughout the entire session.

Subliminal programs have the probability of being played at any time and in any place. You might be listening to these messages while you are working. The best part is that you will not have to stop the task that you are doing and sit down and relax like the way it happens with NLP. Sometimes, subliminal programs will be added to your daily hypnotic programs.

The application of subliminal programming isn't that common. Most people will not select this method to change their habits and behaviors. Research has demonstrated that subliminal programs aren't that effective and so they will not manage to replace NLP.

Despite the portrayal of hypnosis by the media, it is not a bad thing that is meant to take over the minds of unwilling subjects. If the subject is not ready to go through hypnosis, it is impossible to make them get into the altered state. Usually, the application of hypnosis is to make others enhance their lives.

This could be in the form of weight management, quitting smoking, improving other health situations, and helping with chronic pain management. Each of the following techniques is useful in assisting the subject in achieving their general goal.

While all of them can be effective, the professional that you select to work with will be used to define which of these methods will best suit your needs and boost your life.